Includes instructional DVD

PICTUREYOURSELF
Decorating Cakes

Sandy Doell and Linda Shonk

ISBN-10: 1-59863-440-2

ISBN-13: 978-1-59863-440-2

Library of Congress Catalog Card Number: 2007936028

Printed in the United States of America

08 09 10 11 12 BU 10 9 8 7 6 5 4 3 2 1

Publisher and General Manager, Thomson Course Technology PTR:
Stacy L. Hiquet

Associate Director of Marketing:
Sarah O'Donnell

Manager of Editorial Services:
Heather Talbot

Marketing Manager:
Jordan Casey

Acquisitions Editor:
Mitzi Koontz

PTR Editorial Services Coordinator:
Erin Johnson

Copy Editor:
Heather Kaufman Urschel

Interior Layout:
Shawn Morningstar

Interior Photography:
Leslie Mastin

Cover Designer:
Mike Tanamachi

Cover Photos:
Leslie Mastin

DVD-ROM Producer:
Omni Productions

Indexer:
Larry Sweazy

Proofreader:
Sara Gullion

Thomson Course Technology PTR,
a division of Thomson Learning Inc.
25 Thomson Place
Boston, MA 02210
http://www.courseptr.com

Sandy: For my mother, Juanita Hause, whose red cake
is a work of art infused with love and tender care;
no one will ever be able to make it like she does.

Linda: To my loving husband, Gary, who has always
supported me in the pursuit of my dream, and to the memory
of my mother, Ruth Schultz, whose love and encouragement were
with me while writing this book.

Acknowledgments

WE BOTH HAD A LOT OF FUN writing this book. From the day we met to map out a plan and decide on recipes and techniques to include, to the final photo shoot and last-minute phone calls about a pastry tube tip or the name of a tool, we enjoyed not only collaborating to write this book but also rekindling a friendship that began in the hectic business of catering about 25 years ago. At that time, Linda worked from her home, baking and decorating wedding cakes and delivering them every Saturday morning to hotels and country clubs around town. Her fame spread by word of mouth, her talent grew, and she moved up through the ranks of the culinary arts to become the honored chef, teacher, instructor, and business owner/inventor that she is today.

Meanwhile, Sandy's career took a totally different track, and she left catering to work in publishing. Occasionally, a need would arise for a special cake, and her first thought was always, "Call Linda Shonk."

When you work as a caterer, you quickly learn which artists, chefs, decorators, photographers, and florists are the ones you'd call when you need someone to provide those services for your own events. And most of the people who work in catering in Indianapolis would call Linda when they need a cake. Indeed, Linda's cakes have been served at events sponsored by and for the Indiana Pacers and the Indianapolis Colts. She baked the cake that was served at the celebration dinner for the team after their 2007 Super Bowl victory.

When the staff at the country club where Sandy worked all those years ago slowed down after a hectic day of setting up and serving dinner to several wedding receptions in several different rooms, they would often gather in a deserted ballroom to talk about the day's events, finally catch a break to eat something, and maybe taste some of the fancy food served in the rooms they'd been working. A frequent comment at those gatherings was, "Anyone want some wedding cake? There's a Linda Shonk cake in the Evergreen Room." With a cake from every bakery in town, the highest prized cake in the building, by the folks in the business, was always the "Linda Shonk cake."

So when Sandy was approached about writing a book called *Picture Yourself Decorating Cakes*, her first thought, again, was, "Call Linda Shonk."

Sandy did call Linda, not sure she'd have time for the project, not sure she'd have any interest, and not even quite sure she'd remember who Sandy was...and it was as if she'd been waiting for the call. Linda wanted to write a book in which to share some of her cakes and the techniques for making them with others. So Sandy and Linda began a collaboration, the results of which you hold in your hand.

We'd both like to thank Leslie Mastin for working long hours over several days to take most of the photographs featured in this book. The props, the lighting, the camera work—that's all Leslie.

(Except for a few here and there, which Sandy takes all the blame for—those are Sandy in her own kitchen, trying to demonstrate how to break an egg and measure sugar and a few of the procedural shots in Chapters 4 and 5 of Linda demonstrating how to make butterflies and violets—the final product shots are all Leslie, and they're fantastic.) Leslie's skills as a photographer are inspiring, and her contribution enhanced our vision of the book. She took the pictures we knew we wanted and seemed to know instinctively how to get them "just right."

We'd also like to thank Mitzi Koontz for having faith in both of us and for her artistic contributions to the photography work too. She stuck with us through the actual work of writing and photographing this book, once more giving more than an acquisitions editor is required to give. She took a personal interest, and that interest helped us make the book what it is—personal, straightforward, and written and photographed so the beginner can understand how to follow our instructions.

Along with Mitzi, Heather Urschel did more than is required of a copy editor. They both served as our "beginner" audience, questioning us when we used too much jargon or skipped over instructions that they told us beginners needed. We appreciate both of them for their feedback, not to mention just doing their jobs of managing the project and copy editing the text.

Shawn Morningstar has done a wonderful job creating the layout for the book, as she always does, changing the design from chapter to chapter to create the different "looks" necessary, as we moved from the recipes to the instructional material for decorating in the later chapters. She is an artist in her own right.

Sara Gullion and Larry Sweazy, proofreader and indexer, provided exceptional work in a short amount of time. They are much appreciated. Sara saved us from some potentially embarrassing mistakes in the text, and Larry created an index that makes it easy for the reader to find just the recipe or just the instruction needed at the flip of a page.

Linda, in particular, would like to acknowledge her son Joe for his love and patience, going way beyond his current job as manager of Sweet Art Galleries, enhancing his duties as only a loving son could. Joe was there with me as a young boy, helping deliver those cakes to country clubs and hotels and taking more than a passing interest in Mom's job. He looked forward every week to the Saturday morning cake delivery, when he could help the catering staffs with tablecloths and silver polishing and where they taught him all sorts of interesting skills a boy of 8 wants to know, such as napkin folding.

Also to the staff and friends at Ivy Tech College, who have always given me confidence and encouragement. Special thanks to David Hammond, who is more than an employee; he's a true friend who, with his expertise and dedication to quality, has worked tirelessly to ensure that every aspect of my vision is met every day. And finally, a special thanks to Sandy Doell, whose guidance and expertise has made writing this book a pleasurable experience.

Sandy would like to acknowledge her own sons and grandsons, Doug, Bruce, David, Scott, Jonathon, Jimmy, and Timothy, who all served as taste testers for all the cakes that had to be baked in order to write this book. They willingly helped dispose of the evidence once again. Thanks to all my family who gave up holidays and weekends, and who helped take up the slack in my personal responsibilities so that I could, yet again, become obsessed with a book to write. And, of course, thanks to Linda, the very best in the business.

About the Authors

Sandy Doell is the author of *Picture Yourself Planning Your Perfect Wedding* (Thomson Course Technology PTR, November 2007) and a freelance book editor and writer. She has served in many roles in publishing and has edited hundreds of books, most recently *301 Inkjet Tips and Techniques: An Essential Printing Resource for Photographers* by Andrew Darlow.

She is the author of *Mom's Field Guide: What You Need to Know to Make It Through Your Loved One's Military Deployment* (Warrior Angel Press, October 2006). That book is based on her experiences when her son, David, was deployed to Iraq with the U.S. Army in 2004. She has been interviewed by dozens of radio hosts around the country, discussing the needs of the troops and their families, and, along with Warrior Angel Press, she maintains two web sites (momsfieldguide.com and whileourchildrenserve.com) in support of the families of deployed military personnel.

Linda Shonk is the developer of Choco-Pan® rolled icing and an A.C.F.-certified Executive Pastry Chef. Linda has owned and operated both retail and wholesale bakeries since 1974 and is a highly sought after culinary instructor. She teaches students at Sweet Art, Inc. (her place of business in Indianapolis), Ivy Tech Community College in Indianapolis, and travels around the United States giving classes and seminars on a wide variety of topics and techniques. She has also been a guest instructor at Indiana University, Purdue University, International Sugar Art in Atlanta, and Cal-Java International in Los Angeles.

Linda has received many awards and much praise for her work as a culinary artist, including A.C.F. gold, silver, and bronze medals and the prestigious Concepts In Food award. In addition to her work as an instructor, Linda has appeared on *Food Network Challenge*, and her product Choco-Pan® has made an impact on the rolled icing market and has shattered the stereotypes of rolled fondant in general.

Table of Contents

Introduction

" THIS BOOK IS INTENDED TO introduce the pleasures of baking and cake decorating to those with the desire to learn. I have included many of my favorite recipes, techniques, and secrets to make decorating cakes fun. I hope everyone who reads this book can learn something useful to them and become a better baker, cake decorator, or confectionery artist."

—Linda Shonk, American Culinary Federation–certified Executive Pastry Chef

Why We Wrote This Book and Who We Wrote It For

This book is designed to introduce you, the beginner at cake decorating and baking, to the simple pleasures of creating a work of art in your own kitchen and getting the applause, the oohs and aahs, and the admiration of your family and guests. It's a primer on cake decorating, a place to begin if you think you might be interested in a career in the cake decorating business, and a teaching tool for those who just want to learn how to turn out pleasing, delicious cakes that satisfy the eye as well as the taste buds.

We both love cooking, baking, experimenting, and just generally playing with food. Linda, in fact, has made a career of it. Sandy is more the inspired amateur type. Both of us know our way around a kitchen, and we both love baking. Over the years we've discovered what tastes good, what looks good, and a lot of techniques and ways of achieving that good-looking, good-tasting, beautiful dessert called

a cake. This book is the result of our combined years of experimenting and learning, often through trial and error, not to mention the things we learned in our mothers' kitchens many years ago. In this book, we share with you what we've learned about baking and decorating some fairly simple cakes, using buttercream, cream cheese, royal, and fondant icings. The techniques we share here are simple, yet striking in their effect.

Of course, decorating a cake begins with baking one, and we also share here our favorite recipes for cakes. We both grew up with mothers who were artists in the kitchen, so we thought everyone baked cakes, cookies, pies, and bread all the time. We had no idea that this thing that seemed a natural part of daily life to us was something not many people know how to do anymore. We want to change that; we want everyone to know how much fun and how easy it is to bake and decorate cakes. It's truly a win-win situation too—even your mistakes will be tasty, and your family will be more than willing to help you get rid of the mishaps as well as the triumphs.

How This Book Is Organized

In Chapter 1, "Pantry Basics," you'll find a guide to shopping for ingredients for cakes: the flours, sugars, fats, liquids, and flavorings that are combined in varying proportions to create each unique confection. In Chapter 1, we share with you what we know about how to shop for these things, what to buy and what not to buy, and why "from scratch" is the best way to bake a cake.

In Chapter 2, "Tools of the Trade," we talk about mixers, sifters, measuring cups, and a few more advanced tools, such as icing combs and offset spatulas, that make the art of baking and decorating so much easier to do. In any pursuit, the right tool is the key to success, and baking is no exception.

The fun begins in Chapter 3, "Baking the Cakes." This is where you'll learn how to put the ingredients of Chapter 1 together, using the tools you read about in Chapter 2, to create some of the best tasting cakes you'll ever try. Chapter 3 features the cake and frosting recipes we used as a base for the cakes we demonstrate decorating in Chapters 4 and 5.

As a bonus, at the end of Chapter 3, you'll find some good plain cakes that you just bake in a 9"×13" pan and pour the icing on. Nothing fancy—just a couple of good-tasting, simple desserts. These are cakes we bake all the time for our families. We love them, and we know you will too.

In Chapter 4, "Simple Decorating Techniques," we show you how to dress up a cake using simple tools and techniques that anyone can master, even the very beginning cook. Simply stacking up piles of berries on top of a cake and dusting the whole thing with confectioner's sugar is a decorating technique that doesn't require any special skills or even much concentration. Just frost the cake and pile on the berries. Here we teach you how to swirl and smooth frost a cake and how to make some simple decorations using fresh flowers, ribbons, and fresh fruit. We also show you how to make and use a pastry bag and create some simple decorations using buttercream and cream cheese frosting.

Here Linda shares some of her methods for making such decorative items as strawberry tuxedos and petits fours. Her petits fours method is unlike any other, and the results are beautiful tiny filled cakes, coated in chocolate, that look like a team of pastry chefs worked all day to create them.

In Chapter 5, "Decorating Cakes Using Fondant and Royal Icing," you'll learn how to work with royal icing and fondant to create really professional-looking works of art. Linda shares her trick for making folds in a fondant "baby blanket" to cover a shower cake and how to use more specialized tools, such as flower and leaf plungers and textured rolling pins, to create really advanced-looking cakes. You'll also learn some more techniques for working with buttercream, such as creating a rose using a flower nail.

What's On the DVD

On the DVD that accompanies this book, you'll meet Linda Shonk, pastry chef and sugar artist, face to face and watch as she leads you step by step through the application and molding of her Choco-Pan® fondant to create a beautiful rose and daisy fondant cake that looks too good to eat. But you will love eating it because it's all based on the delicious recipes from Chapter 3.

Linda shows you just how easy it is to work with Choco-Pan® and what delightful artwork you can create with it.

Pantry Basics

Before you can decorate a cake, you must bake a cake. Many people are intimidated by the idea of cake baking and wouldn't think of diving into the flour bin and the sugar canister with a measuring cup and a wooden spoon. Many of us would rather let Betty Crocker, Duncan Hines, or the Pillsbury Doughboy handle the details of baking for us. If you prefer cake mixes, you can still decorate your cake and it will still be the highlight of your party. But if you want your family and guests to rhapsodize over your creation, make it "from scratch." Nothing from a box will ever taste nearly as good as the recipes we share with you later in this book.

We want to emphasize that baking is itself an art form. Yes, you can dump a box of premixed powder, a couple of eggs, and some oil into a bowl; stir it all up and pour the mixture into a pan; and then bake it in the oven you preheated to 350 degrees and spread some canned icing on top of it after it cools. Mixing all those dry ingredients yourself and using the proper shortening and just the right amount of leavening agent, however, produces a better, more flavorful cake, a cake you can truly be proud of, and one that just plain tastes better than anything you can produce out of a box.

Leaving out all the preservatives and unpronounceable chemicals that are added to cake mixes to keep the dry stuff from sticking together means that you are a bit closer to organic too, and even though any cake is still a high fat, high sugar content, pastry, if you use fresh ingredients, yours will be more healthful than if you make it from a box of chemicals. Read the labels on the mixes and then read the recipes in this book. If you make the mix yourself, you will be adding sugar, eggs, milk, and butter instead of high fructose corn syrup or partially hydrogenated soybean and/or cottonseed oil. And it's hard for us to even imagine exactly what soy lecithin could possibly add to the flavor of a cake.

I F YOU GREW UP IN THE KIND of kitchens where we both learned to bake (and to eat), you'll be comfortable with all the grocery items discussed in this chapter. If you've never baked a cake before, though, it's not too late. Go to the baking aisle, the same one where, at eye level, you find all the cake mixes and cans of frosting. You'll need to look up and then look down; the top shelf and the bottom one are where you'll find most of the ingredients you need to make a "real" cake.

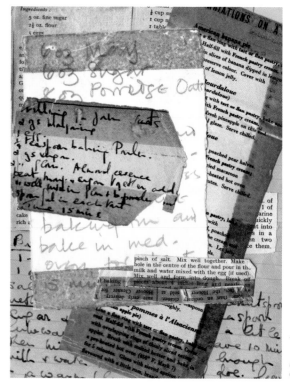

Real life tip from Sandy

As the mother of four sons and the grand-mother of three, I've had some experience satisfying unstoppable appetites. When I bake a cake using fresh ingredients and my own tried and true recipe, if more than two of my sons or grandsons are around, it can be devoured over the course of an evening. But when I've used a cake mix, I've noticed that the cake I bake tends to hang around for a while. They'll eat it, maybe they'll all have a piece, but they leave some on their plates and don't come back looking for more an hour later. It is still there the next day and maybe the day after that. If you want to impress your family, if you want them to dream about your cooking when they are all grown up and live far away, if you just want to see the cake you put effort into appreciated and...well...eaten, make your cake from simple basic ingredients, not from a mix. It isn't that much more difficult and it doesn't dirty any more pans and dishes.

Here then, is an ingredients primer, the kind of stuff you are probably already familiar with and no doubt have on hand. Let's just check to make sure you understand the various forms these ingredients take and which ones are preferred for our purposes. In this chapter you'll learn a few basic principles of chemistry and how these ingredients work together in the heat of the oven. You'll also learn about preferred brand names and shopping for staples and fresh ingredients.

© James Blinn

A cake recipe is an instruction for a chemical reaction. As beginning bakers, we were just given instructions to sift, mix, cream, and bake. And that's still all you really need to know, but we'll take some time here to explain the chemical reaction that results when you follow a basic cake recipe.

Most cakes require the following ingredients:

- **Flour**, the glue that holds the whole thing together. In fact, flour contains an element called *gluten*, which binds the other ingredients together.

- **Sugar** to make your final product sweet, tender, and moist and to join with the fat and spread it throughout the batter.

- **Leavening agents**—baking powder, baking soda, cream of tartar—to create the gas bubbles that make your cake rise.

- **Fat**, in the form of shortening, butter, margarine, or cream, to give your cake flavor and to make it tender, moist, and rich.

Milk and buttermilk provide moisture and flavor and help to bind everything together; they also add some fat content, and in the case of buttermilk, acidity, which helps with leavening and adds an indescribably rich and unique flavor when used in a chocolate cake recipe.

Eggs, which help with flavor, leavening, moisture, and protein content to give the cake a richness it wouldn't otherwise have.

Flavorings and extracts, vanilla, chocolate, and others, which add that little extra fillip of taste that we so appreciate. Some forms of chocolate also add to the fat content of the recipe.

Food coloring, which comes in several forms. This is more likely to be an ingredient in icing, and when using the liquid food coloring most of us are familiar with, the recipe will allow for the extra liquid. We will discuss food coloring in more detail when we talk about decorating the cakes with colored icing.

Salt, to add a counterpoint to the sweetness of the sugar. You want your cake to have character, personality, and good taste. Salt in the recipe provides that and acts to balance the sweetness of the sugar and to tone it down a bit.

Salt and sugar are like point and counterpoint in any recipe, be it a pastry or a vegetable dish. You are probably accustomed to seeing a small amount of salt included in pastry or dessert recipes, but did you know that a pinch of sugar provides more character in a savory dish? If a recipe, such as salsa, lists salt as one of its ingredients, try adding just a pinch of sugar too. You will be pleased with the difference it makes.

A *savory* is any dish that is not sweet yet is flavorful. According to *The American Heritage Dictionary*, one meaning of savory is "piquant, pungent, or salty to the taste, not sweet."

Flour

FLOUR IS FOUND ON THE BOTTOM shelf of the baking aisle in most grocery stores, and it's usually packaged in paper bags. You can find many specialty flours, including rye, whole wheat, buckwheat, and others. The kinds we usually use in cakes though are listed here and discussed in the following sections:

- **Self-rising:** *Gold Medal* and *Pillsbury* are the brands you'll see most often in the supermarket.

- **Cake:** Cake flour usually comes in a box. *Swans Down* and *Softasilk* are brand names you'll find in this variety.

- **Pastry:** Pastry flour is available almost exclusively to commercial bakeries.

- **All purpose:** Just flour. Also comes in *Gold Medal* and *Pillsbury* brands as well as store brands and generic. *King Arthur* is a good flour, although it has a slightly higher protein content than others, which might make it more suitable for bread than for cakes and pastries. White Lily is a brand of flour that is found in the southern states; it is softer, has less protein, and is more suitable for making flaky, light biscuits.

© Peter S

The characteristics of flour depend on the variety of wheat from which it is milled. Different areas of the world produce different qualities of wheat. For instance, North America grows Hard Red Spring, Hard Red Winter, Soft Red Winter, Durham, and White wheats. Varieties grown in Europe and France include Recital, Soissons, and Textel, all of which are "softer," or lower in protein, than those grown in North America. Weather conditions, regional restrictions, milling variations, and enrichment processes affect the final product, producing many varieties and slightly different results when used in your recipes.

Understanding these differences will help you determine which products to use in your recipes. For most of the recipes included in this book, we will recommend all purpose flour or cake flour.

We recommend that you buy only name brand flour. There may be little or no difference between the name brands we specify and a store brand that's on sale or a generic brand that's a few pennies cheaper. The problem with the cheaper choice arises because of volume of production and distribution. Name brands sell their product worldwide, so they sell in much greater quantities. This means that their product moves quickly through the chain of distribution. Store brands sell only to their own outlets. They may buy flour in large quantities shortly after it is milled, but then let it sit in warehouses so that the product you end up buying might have been milled as much as two years ago. Buying the name brand ensures a fresher product.

Self-Rising Flour

Self-rising is a white flour to which baking powder and sometimes salt have been added. One asset of self-rising flour is that the baking powder has been uniformly blended with the flour. The catch, however, is that different recipes call for different amounts of baking powder. Another problem you might encounter with self-rising flour is that baking powder can lose its potency over time, so if you buy large quantities of self-rising flour and it sits in your pantry for months, the product will degrade and can affect the quality of your baked goods over time.

Real life tip from Sandy

Nearly every item that we buy on a recurring basis occasionally undergoes a marketing update that includes new packaging. Mayonnaise and salad dressings, peanut butter, jelly, and many other items that once were packaged in glass now are sold almost exclusively in clear plastic unbreakable containers. Things that once were sold in boxes are now packaged in pouches, ready for the microwave. Tuna in an envelope is a great improvement over the cans that had to be drained. Flour (and sugar, too, as a matter of fact) is still sold in the same type of packaging it was sold in 50 years ago when my mother was perfecting some of the recipes in this book. Little has changed in flour packaging over the years.

Flour comes in a simple paper bag, which leaks from its seams and is easily torn. Decades ago, when people used flour to bake bread, cakes, pastries, and cookies just about every day, it was sold in 25- and 50-pound sacks made of cotton. The thrifty housewife of the 30s and 40s often used these "flour sacks" in making clothing for her family. I'm sure cotton flour sacks would not be useful in today's society, but perhaps some packaging specialist should look into repackaging flour and sugar in some less messy, easier to use container.

Here is what the USDA has to say about the nutritional requirements of flour. In fact, they also dictate how flour is to be packaged—in those leaky paper bags—is there a reason for this? There is a lot of leeway in whether you get hard red spring wheat or soft red winter wheat, and that is why certain brands are better for some baking than others. You want softer (less protein) flour for cakes and biscuits and harder (higher protein content) for bread baking.

Wheat Flour (All Purpose Flour)

The all purpose flour shall be milled from wheat of the classes hard red spring, hard red winter, or soft red winter or hard white or soft white wheat, or any combination thereof, as defined in "Official United States Standards for Wheat."

The all purpose flour shall be entoleted and shall conform to the following detailed chemical and physical requirements.

CHEMICAL AND PHYSICAL REQUIREMENTS

	Minimum	Maximum
Iron	20	—-
Protein (NX5.7), % [1]	9.0	—-
Moisture, %	—-	14.0
Ash, %	—-	[2]
Calcium, mg/lb.	500	625
Vitamin A palmitate, IU/lb	8,800	—-
Falling Number [1]	175	350

1/ These limiting values are on a 14.0 percent moisture basis.

2/ Flour prior to calcium enrichment should be straight flour with an ash content not to exceed 0.50 percent (14 percent moisture basis).

PACKAGING

The all purpose wheat flour shall be packaged in five pound paper bags, ten pound paper bags, or 50 kilogram woven polypropylene bags.

Source: USDA:FSA:PDD:EOB
March 2002 (Contact 202-690-3565)

Cake Flour

Cake flour is "weak," or low in gluten, and is made from *soft* wheat (lower in protein content). It has a very soft, smooth texture and is pure white in color. Cake flour is often used for cakes and other delicate baked goods that require low gluten content. The brands Linda prefers are *Softasilk* and *Swans Down.*

Pastry Flour

This type of flour is used in commercial recipes for pies, cookies, biscuits, and muffins. It is also a "weak" flour but slightly stronger than cake flour. You won't find this in your grocery store, but it is available through commercial outlets.

All Purpose Flour

All purpose flour is commonly found in retail markets, but it is not widely used in commercial applications because commercial bakers prefer more exact milling for better, more consistent, results. All purpose flour, as its name implies, works best for general use in your home kitchen. Linda suggests *Gold Medal* or *King Midas* brands.

Instant Flour

Easy mixing or "instant" flour is available for use in making sauces and gravies; it really does help eliminate lumps too. The recipe for icing for the Red Velvet Cake used in this book lists instant flour as an ingredient. You will find instant flour in some grocery stores sold under the brand name *Gold Medal Wondra.* It comes in one pound boxes and even smaller canisters, but you won't need much of it—just a couple of tablespoons works to thicken any sauce, pudding, or that special red velvet icing.

If you are trying any of the recipes in this book at high altitudes, you'll need to make some adjustments. At altitudes greater than 3,500 feet, water boils more quickly and cakes rise higher; sometimes they even "fall," or sink in the middle as a result of rising too quickly, or batter may spill over the sides of the pan. Cakes can also be a bit drier at high altitudes. To counteract this, try the following:

- Use 5% more flour to offset the rising action of the leavening ingredients.

- Use 20% more liquid to offset the added flour and to provide more moisture to counteract the drying effect.

- Set the oven temperature about 25 degrees higher to help set the crust more quickly.

- Use cold water and large, cold eggs.

- Make sure you grease and flour the pans well.

- Set the cake pans in the lower half of the oven and remove the top rack so that if the cake does rise quickly, it won't encounter any obstacles.

- Finally, make sure your oven temperature is calibrated—altitude can actually affect oven temperatures.

Sugars

SUGARS, OR OTHER SWEETENING agents, serve the following purposes in baking:

 Add sweetness and flavor

 Create tenderness by weakening the gluten structure

 Give color to the crust

 Help the product retain moisture, thereby extending its life

 Act as a creaming agent with fats

 Act as a foaming agent with eggs

 Feed the chemical reaction with yeast

confectioner's sugar   granulated sugar   brown sugar

Most sugar used in the United States comes from sugar cane, but beets are also used to make sugar. Chemically, they are identical, but practically, your results in the kitchen may vary. Some old standard recipes produce less desirable results when beet sugar is used. It doesn't brown as well for things like the Burnt Sugar Cake recipe in this book or on top of crème brulee. Some bakers report that when using beet sugar, there are differences in the texture, appearance, and flavor of their baked products, although they are admittedly slight. We recommend that you buy only sugar labeled "pure cane sugar"—because it's that "slight difference in texture, appearance, and flavor" that wins the blue ribbon at the fair, and that's the level of perfection you are aiming for in your cakes.

Granulated Sugar

Granulated sugar is the most familiar form of sugar and the most widely used. It is also found on the lower shelf in the baking aisle. It often is packaged in paper bags just like all purpose or self-rising flour. This is also called *table sugar*, and you can buy it in small packets or even cubes for individual sweetening of beverages. You can buy colored granulated sugar for use in decorating cakes and cookies too.

Super Fine Sugar

Super fine sugar (called *castor sugar* in England) has a much finer grain than granulated sugar. It has been pulverized just a bit more finely, and is preferred by bartenders for drinks containing sugar. This type of sugar is prized for making cakes and cookies because it produces a more uniform batter and supports a higher quantity of fat.

Super fine sugar can usually be replaced in cake recipes by granulated sugar without ill effect. The icing for the Red Velvet Cake recipe in this book calls for super fine sugar, and in that case, it does make a difference.

This type of sugar is less likely to be available on the grocery store shelf, but it is available from Domino and other sugar manufacturers. If you can't find it in the grocery store, go to the service desk and ask the clerks to order it for you. It is available in gourmet grocery stores as well as well-stocked upscale liquor stores. If all else fails, try searching online for retailers who sell this product in reasonable quantities. Finally, if you can't find super fine sugar anywhere, you can make your own by putting some granulated sugar in a food processor and processing it for a minute.

Sanding Sugar

Sanding sugar is commonly used for cookie decoration. It is a coarser sugar than granulated and often comes in colored varieties. Your local grocery store likely has common colors such as red, blue, green, and yellow. Online sources carry dozens of shades and colors in a variety of package sizes. You can find sanding sugar online at KitchenKrafts.com and other sites. It's also available in gourmet baking stores.

Confectioner's Sugar

Confectioner's, or powdered, sugar is ground to a fine powder and mixed with 3% corn starch to prevent caking. These sugars are graded according to fineness by a number followed by an X. The number represents the number of times it has been sifted, creating a finer texture each time. 12X confectioner's sugar is the finest available, but 10X and 6X are the most common.

Brown Sugar

Brown sugar is a cane sugar that has not been completely refined. The more impurities it contains, the darker the color. Common impurities consist of caramel or molasses. Brown sugar is used in some recipes to replace all or part of the sugar and to impart a different flavor or color to the final product. This variety of sugar contains some acid and, when combined with baking soda, this can affect the leavening process. Always store brown sugar in an airtight container to preserve freshness, and don't buy in large quantities unless you use it often. It is usually sold in one-pound boxes, although you can also find it in two-pound plastic bags. Dark and light brown sugar can be used interchangeably in recipes, depending on the color and flavor you want—or just depending on what's available in your pantry. Both result in a sweet and tasty finished product. This is not the same thing as turbinado sugar. Turbinado is granulated sugar that has not had all the impurities removed. It retains a brown color, but does not have quite the same taste as regular brown sugar.

Leavening Agents

BAKING POWDER, BAKING SODA, and yeast are the catalysts that cause the chemical reaction that results in all the baked goods we love, be they breads, cakes, or other pastries. Most cakes use baking powder because it produces a lighter, more airy product, but many cake recipes, especially chocolate ones, also call for baking soda. For these ingredients, you must look to the top shelf in the baking aisle. Common brands are *Clabber Girl* and *Rumford* baking powder and *Arm & Hammer* baking soda (the same stuff you put in the back of the fridge to keep it smelling fresh).

Baking powder (often designated as "double acting") and baking soda (sodium bicarbonate) are chemical leavening agents. Baking powder is usually just baking soda (an alkali) with at least one acidic leaving agent, such as sodium aluminum sulfate, added. It's called *double acting* if it contains two acids, one of which reacts at room temperature and begins to make a cake batter rise as soon as it is added to the mixture, and another, which doesn't begin to act until the batter is placed into the higher temperature of the oven.

This is where the whole chemical process gets really interesting, and it demonstrates the reason you must measure exactly and follow a recipe's instructions as exactly as possible without making substitutions. The first instruction of almost any cake recipe tells you to "cream together" a measurement of shortening or butter with some type of sugar. When you do this, small *seed bubbles* are created. When you later add the leavening agent to your chemical process, it begins to work on those tiny bubbles, making them expand. The action of the heat on the "high temperature" leavening agent makes those bubbles expand a bit more, and then the heat quickly works to set those bubbles in size as the batter becomes firm in the oven—and magically turns into cake.

Further complicating the reaction of salts and acids that make your cake rise is the acid and fat content of the milk, cream, or chocolate product that you use in your recipe. Buttermilk is itself an acidic agent, so when recipes call for buttermilk, some of the baking powder, with its higher acid content, is often replaced by baking soda, an alkaline ingredient.

Real life tip from Sandy

Buttermilk and baking soda are two familiar ingredients in most of the chocolate cake recipes I've inherited from my mother, an excellent southern cook from Alabama. In most cake recipes, leavening agents are mixed with flour and salt and then added alternately with milk or another liquid to a sugar/shortening/egg mixture. When a southern cook's recipe for chocolate cake calls for buttermilk, it almost invariably also calls for baking soda. And my mother's instructions indicate that the soda should be mixed with the buttermilk before it's added to the rest of the batter. Don't do this until you are ready to add the buttermilk to the batter, though, because the alkali and the acid begin to work together almost immediately, and the buttermilk starts to "swell" in the measuring cup. I don't know why this makes chocolate cakes taste better, but trust me: it does.

Fats

FATS ARE USED IN BAKED GOODS for the following reasons:

- To tenderize the product and soften texture
- To add moisture and richness
- To extend the life of the final product
- To add flavor

Expert tip from Linda

Many types of fat are available. Each one has different properties that make it suitable for different purposes. As a baker, you must consider the melting points of each fat, the degrees of hardness in its various stages, its flavor, and its ability to form emulsions.

Regular shortening has a tough, waxy texture and the small particles of fat tend to hold shape in dough or batter. These shortenings can be manufactured to various degrees of hardness. Regular shortenings have a good creaming ability, which means a good quantity of air can be incorporated, giving them lightness and leavening power. These are usually used in flaky products such as pie crust, biscuits, and cookies. Unless another type of shortening is specified, always use regular shortening.

The recipes in this book call for either butter or shortening. When a recipe calls for butter, you should use unsalted stick butter. You can usually substitute stick margarine with a fat content of 80% (the same as butter), but butter is butter—a dairy product. Animal fat—lard, bacon grease, or beef suet—is not recommended for baked goods. Use shortening, butter, or margarine as specified in each recipe.

Emulsified Shortening

These are soft shortenings that spread easily throughout a batter and quickly coat particles of sugar or flour. Because they contain added emulsifiers, they will hold larger quantities of liquid and sugar, allowing for a product that is more moist and finely textured. These shortenings do not cream well. If a recipe calls for creaming ingredients, regular shortening should be used.

Expert tip from Linda

When the weight of sugar within a recipe is greater than the weight of flour, it is referred to as a *high ratio* formula. When this occurs, emulsified shortening should be used. Because of this, emulsified shortenings are sometimes called high ratio shortenings.

Real life tip from Sandy

The most readily available shortening and the one found in nearly every kitchen I've ever entered is *Crisco*. If the recipes in this book call for shortening, *Crisco* is the brand I use and it works fine. You can use the kind that comes in a can or the new type that comes in sticks, like margarine. Sometimes it's "butter flavored," but I always just use the plain old white stuff in the can. Yes, it is partially hydrogenated, and it's a trans fat, but consider: A typical recipe calls for $\frac{2}{3}$ cup of shortening and makes a cake that will serve 12 to 14 people. Do the math if you want to, but that's not a lot of trans fat per serving, and it is okay to indulge once in a while.

Use *Crisco*, and under no circumstances should you substitute oil for shortening; if a recipe says shortening, it means the stuff that is solid at room temperature. To measure shortening, use a dry measuring cup, press it into the cup firmly to remove any air bubbles and use a straight knife or spatula to make it level with the top of the cup. For easy removal from the measuring cup, hold the bottom of the cup under hot running water for a minute. The shortening will slide out easily.

Butter

Butter is a natural product containing approximately 80% fat, 15% water, and 5% milk solids. It has a very desirable flavor and is available in salted and unsalted varieties. For a fresh, sweet taste in your baked goods, unsalted butter is preferred. If salted butter is used, less salt may be needed in your recipe.

Margarine

Margarine is manufactured from various hydrogenated animal and vegetable fats, plus flavorings. Margarine contains 80% fat, 15% moisture, and 5% milk solids and is considered imitation butter. You must be careful when purchasing margarine because the whipping methods and flavors used can give very different results depending on the brand. We recommend *Imperial* or I *Can't Believe It's Not Butter* brands of margarine, but other brands will do. Just make sure you don't pick up anything labeled "whipped" or "light" or any of the varieties that have substituted air or water for some of the fat content in the product. This is great stuff for spreading on bread or muffins, but it will negatively affect your baked goods. Never use in your cake recipes the "spreadable directly from the fridge" types of margarine that come in tubs. Use the stick kind that is hard when refrigerated but soft when left at room temperature.

Creams, Milk, and Buttermilk

MANY TYPES OF CREAMS AND milks are available for use in your recipes. Following is a list with the fat content of each product. It's the fat content that determines each dairy product's best use.

Heavy Whipping Cream	36–40% fat	Best for toppings
Light Whipping Cream	30–35% fat	Usually best if cream is used in a recipe
Light Cream	16–22% fat	Sometimes called table cream or coffee cream. Not to be confused with Light Whipping Cream
Half & Half	10–12% fat	Just what it says it is: half milk and half cream.
Milk	4% fat	Also called whole milk. You might be tempted to substitute 2%, 1%, or even skim in recipes, but the lower fat content will affect your final product. When a recipe in this book calls for milk, you should use whole milk for best results.
Buttermilk		Fresh liquid skim milk that has been cultured or soured by bacteria. Buttermilk has a special use in chocolate cakes of all sorts.
Sour Cream		Cream that has been cultured by adding lactic acid bacteria. It contains about 18% fat and holds moisture in baked goods. It also gives body to cake and muffin recipes. Sour cream also works well with chocolate.
Evaporated Milk		This is whole or skim milk with 60% of the water removed. It is then sterilized and canned.
Condensed Milk		This is whole or skim milk with 60% of the water removed. It is heavily sweetened and heated to dissolve sugar. It has a much heavier consistency than evaporated milk.

Do not confuse the last two items in this list. Evaporated milk and condensed milk are two different things. Evaporated milk is sold under the brands *Carnation* and *Pet*. The most commonly known brand of condensed milk is *Eagle Brand Milk*. You will find both in the baking aisle of the grocery store.

Eggs

WHEN USING EGGS, always be aware of freshness dates and make sure eggs are stored properly in a cooler or refrigerator. All recipes in this book will be based on Grade A Whole Large Eggs unless otherwise specified.

© Lisa Eastman

In baking, eggs perform the following functions:

Structure	Egg protein coagulates to give structure to baked products. This is very important in high ratio cakes where high sugar and fat contents weaken the gluten that holds the batter together.
Emulsifying Fat and Liquids	Eggs contain natural emulsifiers which help to produce smooth batters. This also contributes to better volume and texture.
Leavening	Beaten eggs incorporate air in tiny cells or bubbles. In batter, the air expands when heated, thus helping the leavening process.
Shortening Action	The fat in egg yolks can act as a shortening. This is important for products low in other fats.
Moisture	Eggs are mostly water and are calculated as part of the total liquid in recipes.
Flavor	Eggs add richness and enhance the flavor of sweet pastries.
Nutritional Value	Eggs are an excellent source of protein.
Color	Egg yolks are very important to the color of baked goods. Many items, such as bread and pie crusts, use egg wash (egg yolks blended with water or milk) to improve color and visual appeal.

Flavorings

MOST WHITE OR YELLOW CAKE recipes call for a teaspoon of vanilla. This can be either imitation or an actual extract from the vanilla bean. We usually use and prefer imitation vanilla, which is less expensive than the extract. We do recommend, however, for reasons we've mentioned before, that you buy a name brand. In many store chains, it's hard to find name brands of flavorings and spices. Go to a store that stocks *McCormick's* or *Durkee's* brands. The large supermarkets often seem to sell only their own brands of these items, and for most people, that may be "good enough," but for you, who wants your cakes to be famed among family and friends...well, you'll want to go out of your way to find an independent grocery that stocks a better brand.

Occasionally, a cake will call for almond or lemon flavoring. Again, all we have to add is "buy the name brand." A new development is clear vanilla flavoring, without color. We haven't tried this yet, but it should be an asset for white cakes.

Chocolate and Cocoa

Cocoa is the dry powder that remains after part of the cocoa butter is removed from chocolate liquor. *Hershey's* cocoa is the brand we use when our recipes call for cocoa.

Dutch processed cocoa is processed with an alkali. It is slightly darker and smoother than natural cocoa, and it also dissolves more easily into liquids than natural cocoa. A few familiar brands of Dutch processed cocoa are *Hershey's*, *Dutch Boy*, and *Ghirardelli*.

Natural cocoa is acidic. When natural cocoa is used in recipes, it can be mixed with baking soda. Natural cocoa contains no added sugar and has a more intense chocolate flavor. It is available in health food stores and in specialty stores (or online). This is the kind of chocolate you want to use in Devil's Food Cake recipes when you want the richest chocolate flavor available.

Chocolate liquor is totally unsweetened chocolate that contains no sugar and has a very bitter taste. It is used to flavor things that have other sources of sweetness. Chocolate liquor usually gives a very rich chocolate taste to things like brownies and flourless chocolate cakes and tortes.

The recipes in this book will distinguish which chocolate or cocoa should be used for the most successful result.

Your Pantry

W HEN YOU GO SHOPPING FOR ingredients, buy exactly what is called for in your recipe and buy the very best brands available. It's okay to buy generic or store brand paper plates, but for your cake recipes, and indeed, for all your cooking, start with the very best and freshest ingredients and don't substitute. Each item called for in each recipe is calculated to produce a desired effect in a chemical reaction. You don't want to go to the effort of baking a cake and sabotage your hard work with substandard or wrong ingredients. It isn't hard to bake if you start by exercising exacting standards in the grocery store.

2

Tools of the Trade

The most important tool you can bring to any creative endeavor is your imagination—or someone else's. You could just mark the occasion of someone's birthday, graduation, or anniversary celebration with the traditional "Happy Birthday, Ben" or "Congratulations, Sophie," but by using the skills we'll teach you in this book, you can mark each celebration in a unique way that means something special to the guest of honor. Almost any occasion you celebrate is appropriate for a special cake of some kind. Think of what's important to the guest of honor and then find a way to incorporate that hobby or interest into the theme for your cake. For that, you'll need your imagination... and a few other things.

THE TOOLS WE DESCRIBE HERE ARE available in upscale kitchen stores, craft stores, and from online suppliers. If you've tried baking before and thought you weren't very good at it, check to make sure you are using the correct tools, get your kitchen cabinets resupplied, and then try again. The right tool does make you a better craftsperson.

Before you begin any creative work, you need to plan ahead. If you were painting a picture or cross stitching a wall hanging, you'd want to tailor your piece to fit the wall it's going to hang on, or you might have in mind a place to display each piece as you create it. When you start to create a decorated cake, the first thing you must do is visualize the finished product. How big will it be? What color scheme will the decorations be? Answering these questions will help you decide which dish or display method to use for your masterpiece, and that will help you to decide which size pan you'll want to bake the cake in.

If you are just baking a nice cake for immediate family to enjoy tonight, a cake carrier or even just a dinner plate or large round platter will work just fine. For your own fun though (and just for practice), you might want to consider presentation, even if all you plan is a nice dessert as a treat for your family. Are you thinking about a special cake you want to bake next month for your sister's birthday? You can always practice making roses or daisies on the cake you're baking tonight for your family. There's one great thing about cake decorating—you won't need to rip out the stitches and start over after you try something that doesn't work. Someone will always be happy to help you dispose of your mistakes.

Besides, if you own a pedestal stand or a crystal cake plate, why leave it gathering dust in the cabinet or on a shelf? Use it even when baking just for your family. What more important people will you ever feed? Everyone tastes first with their eyes, so presentation is a key part of the dessert experience you want to create.

Basic Pans and Baking Equipment

YOU PROBABLY ALREADY HAVE most of these tools—measuring cups, baking pans, and rolling pins—in your kitchen. Others are more specialized but still available at ordinary consumer outlets like Michael's, Williams-Sonoma, and Sur la Table. A few are highly specialized, but they make all the difference in giving your decorations a really finished, professional-looking touch.

Measuring Cups and Spoons

If you're roasting a chicken and the instructions say to add two tablespoons of parsley and a teaspoon of salt, it really won't matter much if you get a little less or a little more. Baking, however, is based on chemical reactions and moisture content, and measuring must be precise. If a recipe calls for 1/4 teaspoon of salt, the finished product will be affected if you leave the salt out—not just the taste but perhaps the height to which the cake rises or the relative moisture of the "crumb." You want your baked goods to turn out County Fair Perfect each time, so use good measuring tools and measure carefully.

Measuring cups come in two varieties—a glass or plastic cup with measurements marked on the side for measuring liquids and plastic or metal cups for measuring dry ingredients. When measuring liquids, set the cup on a level counter, and bring your eyes down to the level of the cup as you measure. Look through the side as you watch to see that the liquid reaches the line on the side of the cup for the measurement you want. If you try to judge this by holding the cup at eye level or by looking at the cup from above, your measurement is likely to be inaccurate. Glass as well as clear liquids can distort vision. Look through the side of the cup as you measure.

For dry ingredients—flour, sugar, and shortening—use a dry measuring cup and level the ingredient with the top of the cup. Do not mound ingredients. Fill the cup with the flour or sugar, then use a spatula to level the ingredient with the top of the cup. Brown sugar and shortening should be packed tightly, pressed down with a spoon or your fingers to make sure no air bubbles are left in the cup.

Measuring spoons come in graduated sizes, usually in ⅛, ¼, ½, ¾, and 1 teaspoon sizes and 1 tablespoon. One tablespoon is equal to three teaspoons. These are used to measure both wet and dry ingredients. Dry ingredients should be leveled off with the top of the spoon to ensure correct measurement.

Waxed and Parchment Paper

Always nice for baking projects, waxed paper does release nicely. Parchment paper is less expensive and stronger, though, and it works better for lining pans and other uses. In the "Petits Fours" chapter, you will learn a simple way to use a plastic fork and a parchment-lined cookie sheet to make coating petit fours and covered candies much easier and less messy, and that will result in a nicer finished product.

Cutting Boards

Cutting boards of all sizes, shapes, and materials are now available. They are all nice, and for once, we won't tell you that one is preferred over another for baking needs. Use one of any material or in any shape or size you want, but by all means, have one handy for cutting, rolling, and just for keeping your pastry area organized.

Pans

You have several choices when it's time to pick out pans to bake your cakes in, and we can help guide you through the process. If you're lucky, you have some old faithful pans that you've had around for a long time. They work well for you, and your cakes turn out dependably well every time you use them. Treasure those pans because they don't make 'em like that any more. Don't ever let them go.

You should have in your kitchen at least three round cake pans, either 8" or 9" in diameter, two rectangular pans (one 11" × 7" and one 13" × 9"), and a couple of 9-inch square pans. Some cupcake or muffin tins will also come in handy when you need something for a picnic or a child's party.

You should also have a tube pan, a springform pan for cheese cakes, and a loaf pan for baking quick breads. You might someday also need an angel food cake pan with a removable bottom, but that's probably for later in your baking career. You'll find all sorts of specialized baking pans such as brioche pans, muffin top pans, silicone pans, and French bread pans, but for the recipes in this book, we'll just be sticking to the basics. Specialty pans are fun too; for the quinceanera cake featured in Chapter 4, we used a set of heart-shaped pans. Aluminum ones are available from many cake decorating suppliers, including Wilton, and in craft stores.

I have always felt that nice, heavy gauge aluminum pans give more uniform baking, and they have a much longer working life than the newer, lighter weight pans. The slightly higher price is well worth it, and in fact, many coated nonstick pans cost more than aluminum and are of inferior quality. Coated pans can give fluctuating results depending on the oven you use and the type of heat you have.

Real life tip from Sandy

I have since baked some angel food cakes in my life that were quite good, but the first I attempted was a disaster. I had just discovered that my newly acquired husband loved angel food cake, his mom gave me her recipe, and he was arriving home that day after a week long trip out of town. I decided to surprise him with a nice welcome home meal, including his favorite dessert. So I dug around in my cabinets and found what looked like an angel food cake pan. I followed the recipe, poured the batter into the pan, put it in the oven, and stood back to await the usual aroma of fresh baked cake.

Then the cake started to rise...and rise...and rise until it started spilling over the sides of the pan. The batter hit the hot aluminum and became something akin to an angel food crisp. Finally, it stopped and what was left in the pan became an edible cake. What I thought was an angel food cake pan, which will hold about 16 cups of batter, in fact was a tube pan, and a small one at that: it held about 9 cups of batter, leaving 7 cups to spill out the sides. I lost a big part of the cake over the sides of the pan and had a big mess to clean up afterward. But still...what came out of the oven that day, in the form of cake or crusty bits from the side of the pan, still tasted good. Even your initial experiments will be eaten.

If you don't have any old trusty pans that you know are your friends, you are still in luck; there are good ones to be had, but you probably won't find what you're looking for at your local department store or discount mall. There's only one kind of pan that will make your cakes turn out the best they can be every time, and that is a pan made of heavy gauge aluminum. And that is difficult to find these days. You can browse around your local discount department store and find all the coated, nonstick, or silicone bakeware you want. All of those sound good, but they are not what professional cooks and really good home cooks use. We use aluminum... heavy gauge aluminum...and it's hard to find nowadays.

All brand new pans must be properly *seasoned* before the first time you use them to assure easy removal of your cake after baking, even the coated ones. Pans can be seasoned by applying a thin coat of shortening to the inner baking surface and placing the pan in a 150–200 degree oven for 30–45 minutes. Be sure to check the label on your pan for more specific seasoning instructions.

Wire Racks

Wire racks are useful for cooling certain cakes (cheesecakes, for instance) that should remain in the pan during the cooling process. If the cake is to be turned out of the pan for cooling, set the pan holding the hot cake on a wire rack, then turn the cake out to place it directly on the rack, a parchment-lined cookie sheet, or even a clean towel.

Spatulas and Smoothing Tools

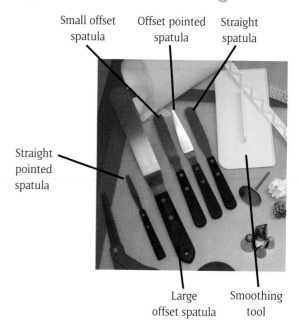

Small offset spatula

Offset pointed spatula

Straight spatula

Straight pointed spatula

Large offset spatula

Smoothing tool

You should keep an assortment of knives and spatulas within easy reach at all times. They are good multi-purpose tools. When icing cakes, you can choose a straight spatula or an offset spatula. This is a personal choice, and you should try both to determine which one works best for you. A long serrated cake knife is a must to trim cakes and make them level; the serration will keep your cake from crumbling. You use smoothing tools as you would a spatula when smoothing buttercream. For fondant, you need a trowel-like tool called a *fondant smoother*.

When it's time to serve your finished cake, always use a serrated cake or bread knife and cut with a short sawing motion. The result will be a clean cut with the layers remaining intact in the cut piece.

Flower Nails and Fondant Cutters

Flower nail Fondant plunger cutters

Floral wire , available from craft shops and florists, is used as a support in hand-made gum paste flowers. If you use floral wire in your decorations, be sure to remove these decorations before you serve the cake—or if someone else will be serving the cake, be sure you tell them to remove all flowers and wire before they begin to serve the cake.

Ribbon is used to accent sugar floral bouquets, or to add color or trim to cakes and cake boards.

You should always make sure that any inedible items used to decorate your cakes are removed before you begin serving. If someone else will be serving the cake, it's your responsibility to inform them of any inedible items they need to remove.

A *flower nail* is a threaded nail with a large flat head. Flower nails are used for making buttercream flowers such as roses, pansies, and mums.

Paint Brushes

Always keep a good assortment of clean, high quality paint brushes on hand. They are great for many uses including:

 Accenting flowers and trim with food coloring or food color dust

 Repairing buttercream and royal icing flowers

 Painting on fondant cakes with food coloring, color dusts, or cocoa

We will demonstrate some ways to use paint brushes in Chapter 5.

Pastry Bags and Tips

Paper pastry tube

Decorating tips

Pastry bags are available in many different materials and sizes. Be sure to read the packaging carefully when selecting these items to be sure you choose a size that fits your hand. If a bag is too big, you won't be able to regulate hand pressure, and borders and other decorations will appear sloppy and uneven.

Canvas bags are easy to use and durable. They can be washed and re-used many times. If you plan to decorate cakes often, you might want to invest in a couple of these.

Disposable bags are available in plastic or vinyl. They too come in many sizes and strengths. They can be refilled a few times for a single project, but afterward they must be discarded.

Decorating tips are some of the most useful tools in your cake decorating toolbox. Standard kits are available in the grocery store or in craft stores at reasonable prices. Quality tips can be purchased individually or in kits; these are available through decorating stores or gourmet shops. Make sure to wash all tips after each use. Store them in a container to protect and keep them organized because they are easy to lose and can be easily damaged. With proper care, you will be able to use the same tips for many years. Tips, sometimes called *tubes,*

are available in many shapes and sizes. Start with the basic four (star, round, petal, and writing) and add specialty tips (grass, rose/star combination, pastry filler, and more) as you need them for specific projects.

A *pastry comb* is a tool to add zig-zags, lines, and curves to the sides of your cake.

Pastry comb

Some other tools that will come in handy as you start to work with icing as an artistic medium on your baked goods are rolling pins, texture pins, edging tools, and scissors. A pastry wheel also comes in handy for maintaining a straight edge as you cut fondant. Rolling pins are useful for rolling out the fondant, and special decorative rolling pins are used to imprint the fondant with a design; edging tools give the cut fondant a finished appearance And scissors come in handy for a variety of tasks.

You can make your own parchment pastry cones from a triangle of parchment paper using a simple coning method. This skill is good to know and you can easily make large or small bags to fit the job at hand. You can also just take a plastic food storage bag, cut a hole in one corner, and attach a pastry tip for a quick disposable pastry bag.

Follow these simple directions:

1. Hold the paper triangle as shown, grasping the center of the long side between the thumb and forefinger of the left hand. Of course, you will reverse these directions if you are left-handed.

2. With the right hand, roll the top corner down to the center of the triangle. Hold the paper in this position with the right hand.

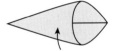

3. With the left hand, roll the bottom corner up to complete the cone.

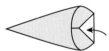

4. Adjust the cone so that the point is completely closed and sharp. Fold down the loose edges of the open end of the cone so that it does not unroll.

5. Fill the cone and fold the open end several times so that it is tightly closed. With scissors, cut off a very small piece of the tip of the cone. Hold the cone between the thumb and fingers as shown.

Before you start to decorate, squeeze out some frosting until you've removed all air bubbles and gotten the flow moving smoothly.

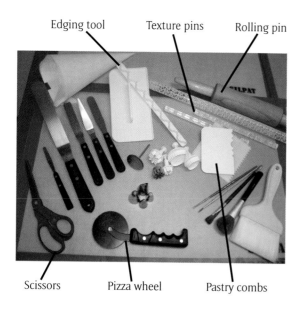

Edging tool   Texture pins   Rolling pin

Scissors   Pizza wheel   Pastry combs

Stands

Cake stands are available in many styles, sizes, shapes, and price ranges. Some serve both as a support structure and as a presentation piece. Others are for display only. Still others are not seen at all but are simply support structures. Consider each cake you make and decide whether a supporting stand is needed. You can buy plastic cake carriers, old-fashioned glass plates with domed metal covers, footed glass or pottery with or without covers—the choices and styles are limitless. This is the presentation part of cake decorating, the part you must plan ahead for. Stands that supply support usually come with columns or dowel rods for you to use. A small, simple cake is happy sitting on a cardboard round covered with foil; wooden dowels can be added for support if the cake is more than two or three layers thick.

Turntables

Turntables are stands that turn easily and allow you to decorate cakes without having to turn the cake with your hands every few seconds. If you like to decorate large cakes, or plan to decorate cakes often, a commercial turntable is a good investment. They are sturdy and easy to care for and clean, are not heavy, and are easy to store. If you don't have a lot of storage space, the small Rubbermaid turntable works well for cakes of less than 10" in diameter, and is affordable.

A Good Mixer

To a professional chef and a serious cook, a powerful mixer is not just a tool; it's an investment. Invest in the best one you can find. Many chefs and home cooks have mixers they've been using for 20 years or more. A handheld electric mixer works for mashing potatoes or stirring up some pudding or a cake from a mix. But if you're serious about baking, you will find a heavy duty mixer on a stand, one with a turntable where you place a heavy glass or metal bowl, actually makes you a better cook.

Buying a mixer is a lot like buying a new car. They're all shiny and pretty, some are sleek, and some look a bit more staid and sturdy. The difference is under the hood. Pay no attention to claims of 10 or 12 speeds. What you want in a mixer is wattage, and you have to dig for that information. Good ones come in ranges from 400 to 1,000 watts and even higher for commercial grade mixers. The higher the wattage, the more powerful the mixer, and the more powerful the mixer, the more you're going to enjoy baking. You'll pay about $200 for a 400-watt mixer and about $500 for a 1,000-watt mixer. Some commercial ones list for $2,000. Shop around and get some power behind your beaters.

If you buy a low wattage mixer and then try to make it grind its way through thick cookie or bread dough, you'll get to watch the sparks fly and then you'll be shopping for a new mixer. If you can afford it, buy the best and it will be a trusty kitchen tool 20, or even 30 or more, years from now.

Tabula Rasa

Having a clean, organized workplace is extremely important. Always review a recipe before you begin and have all your ingredients pre-measured if possible before starting. This way many things can be put away and a larger work space will be available. Once the mixing process is complete and the cake is in the oven, you can begin to clear a space for cooling. Always give yourself ample time for this process. Cooling takes longer for heavier cakes (i.e. carrot cake, cheesecake), and proper cooling/setting time for angel food cake is a must to avoid a fallen cake.

Real life tip from Sandy

Definitely have your work space clean at the beginning of your project. Definitely clean it again after each phase is complete. Clean all mixers, utensils, measuring cups and spoons after you use them; you will be needing them again in a few minutes. I like to review the recipe before I begin just to make sure I have all the ingredients the recipe calls for. I don't pre-measure though. If it helps you stay organized, do it, but I just like to have everything lined up and then measure and mix at the same time.

Real life tip from Sandy

Sometimes it's hard to keep a cookbook open and flat so that you can read from it as you follow a recipe. And you can always find the recipes you use over and over again because those pages are usually splattered and stained from years of use. Cookbook stands are useful for keeping a cookbook open to the page you're using and to keep your cookbooks up off the counter top and out of the path of splatters from the mixer.

It is a simple matter though, to just make copies of your favorite recipes and keep your cookbook out of the line of fire. Just lay that one piece of paper on the counter; it's disposable. I find it comes in handy as a place to set small items, such as measuring spoons or bottles of extracts and colorings; I tend to misplace these as I work, and it helps to have that central spot I return to again and again to read the recipe and pick up my measuring spoons.

Time

Visualize yourself following a recipe before you start to actually make it. This will help you to allot the right amount of time for each step of your project. Measuring and scaling of ingredients can usually be accomplished in 15–20 minutes. Mixing times may vary greatly depending on the number of ingredients and stages of mixing. After your project is mixed, baked, cooled, and decorated, it is good to allow time for your icing to *set*, or form a very slight crust on the outermost layer. This is best accomplished by placing the cake in the refrigerator for at least 30 minutes. The first time you make any recipe, try timing each step as you go. Make notes on the recipe for future reference. You'll make fewer mistakes and there will be less likelihood of damage to your final product if you allow the right amount of time to complete the decorating and time for the cake to set. Following these guidelines will ensure good results every time, and good results boost your personal confidence and help you become an experienced cake decorator.

The right tool for the job is true in nearly every profession. Here are the tools Linda used in making the cakes featured in this book. These are the ones she uses every day in her bakery and in her classes.

3

Baking the Cakes

The recipes we share with you in this book are ones we've both used for years. Some of them were inherited from our mothers, some we've adapted over the years, and some are recent acquisitions or even creations of our own. All have passed the taste test with both of our families and with Linda's clients.

B EFORE YOU begin, there a few terms we use here that you need to be familiar with. If you are an old hand at baking, you can skip this part and go directly to the recipes. If not, read this section to familiarize yourself with the "language of baking."

The Language

 Cream: Do this with sugar and butter. Mix them together, and then beat thoroughly to make sure each little crystal of sugar is carefully coated with fat. This is the point in the recipe where you create those *seed bubbles* we told you about in Chapter 1, "Pantry Basics." Use your electric mixer on high speed for this.

 Sift: Place the sifter in a bowl and measure the dry ingredients into it. To sift together flour, baking powder, and salt, place them one after another into the sifter set in the bowl, and then either crank the sifter handle or tap it against the heel of your hand so that the dry ingredients fall through the sieve at the bottom.

 Fold: Stir together gently using top to bottom strokes to avoid the introduction of any additional air to your mixture. Usually used when adding beaten egg whites to a batter. Do this by hand.

Mix: This is usually the instruction when you are adding flour and other dry ingredients to the sugar/fat/egg mixture to create the final batter. The flour/leavening mixture is usually sifted together to make sure the leavening is evenly distributed in the final batter. Most recipes say that you should add the dry ingredients alternately with the liquid, beginning and ending with the dry ingredients. This is to make sure there are no puddles of moisture or dryness and that all ingredients are mixed together thoroughly. Do this at a medium to medium-high speed on the mixer.

Beat: This means to mix at a high speed. It's pretty much the same thing as *whip*. You beat egg whites to make a meringue.

Whip: To beat or mix at a high speed. Egg whites and whipping cream are whipped to incorporate air into them and make a fluffy, light, airy, and delicate substance.

How Do I...?

Q: How do you know when a cake is done?

A: There are three tests for doneness. One is to gently prod the center of the cake with your finger. Push until you see an indentation, then remove your finger. If the cake rises back up to level, it is done. The second, and our favorite, method is to stick a wooden toothpick directly into the center of the cake. If the toothpick comes out with only a dry crumb or two adhered to it, the cake is done. If it comes out with any moist batter coating it, the cake needs a few more minutes. You should also notice the sides of the cake pulling away from the pan when it is done.

Check for doneness before the cake is expected to be done. If the recipe says to bake the cake for 25 minutes, you should begin checking for doneness after it's been in the oven for 20 minutes. Not all ovens are calibrated perfectly—and sometimes even changes in the humidity from one day to the next can affect baking time.

Q: What's the best way to remove a cake from a pan?

A: We recommend lining the baking pan with parchment. To do this, measure a piece of parchment paper that will fit snugly in the bottom of the cake pan, covering the entire pan. Press the parchment into the bottom of the pan to "mark" it; then cut the paper to fit.

The next step is to grease the bottom and sides of the pan with shortening. Then place the parchment paper in the bottom of the pan and grease it, too. Dust the parchment paper with flour, and the pan is prepared. When the cake is done, let it cool in the pan for five minutes. Then run a knife around the edge if necessary and gently turn the pan upside down on a wire cake rack. Carefully remove the pan from the cake and peel away the parchment paper.

Q: How do you stack a layer cake without tearing the layers?

A: When the cake has completely cooled, place the bottom layer on the platter, cake plate, or dish you plan to serve it on. Put a small dollop of frosting on the plate, then place the first layer. This helps hold the first layer in place while you work to stack the other layers on top of it. Working quickly, spread the first layer with frosting or with one of the fillings we provide recipes for later in this chapter. Continue until you have all layers in place.

Expert tip from Linda

Then place the cake in the freezer for half an hour. This makes the next step much easier to accomplish.

Q: How do I apply a crumb coating to the cake? What is a crumb coating anyway?

A: A crumb coating is a thin layer of frosting applied to the entire cake. Some crumbs will show through in the crumb coating. Consider this like using a primer when you paint. Crumb coating helps to cover the cake and holds the crumbs so that none can escape into the final layer. You should usually use buttercream or cream cheese frosting as your crumb coating. The final frosting can then be more buttercream, cream cheese frosting, or it can be fondant.

Q: What is meant by splitting, or *torteing,* layers?

A: Slicing a cake layer in half makes for thinner layers. This means there will be more layers and that the frosting or filling layers are closer together. It helps to ensure that each bite of cake contains both cake and frosting. It also turns three layers into six, which is just more of a wow factor for you. We demonstrate how to do this in Chapter 4, in the instructions for the Waldorf-Astoria Red Velvet Cake and the Boston Cream Pie.

Real life tip from Sandy

I always make two batches of frosting. It's not much fun trying to cover an entire cake with one cup of frosting when clearly two cups would make the job much easier. Make a batch of whatever frosting you plan to use and crumb coat the cake. Then make another batch and sculpt it onto the cake in swirls and designs of your own. Or make a batch of buttercream frosting to use for the crumb coat and then use one of the other frostings, such as cream cheese or Waldorf-Astoria, for your finishing touches. Think of frosting as painting; it's much easier when you don't have to spread a small amount of paint so that it barely covers a wall. Make another batch!

THESE ARE THE RECIPES we used to make the cakes presented in this book. In this chapter, we present the basic recipes. If you simply follow the directions to bake these cakes, you will be thrilled with the resulting desserts. To make them extra special, though, go to Chapters 4 and 5. There we show you the techniques Linda uses to frost and decorate her beautiful cakes. We walk you through the procedures, and we give you a few suggestions for finding inspiration for your creations.

Burnt Sugar Cake

This is an old-fashioned recipe, one that dates from the late 19th Century when every kitchen boasted a cast iron skillet and baking something that wowed the family was a daily occurrence.

Ingredients:

1½ cups sugar (divided into three half cups)

½ cup boiling water

2 eggs, separated

½ cup butter or margarine, softened

1 teaspoon vanilla

2¼ cups all purpose flour

3 teaspoons baking powder

1 teaspoon salt

1 cup milk

Needed:

Cast iron skillet or heavy copper pot

1 large mixing bowl

2 small mixing bowls

Rubber spatula

Electric mixer

Sifter

Two 9" or three 8" round pans

Parchment paper

Prep time: 20–25 minutes (plus cooling time for syrup)

Baking time: 20–25 minutes (375 degrees F)

Preheat oven to 375F. Set rack in middle of oven. Grease and flour two 9-inch or three 8-inch round layer pans.

1. Heat ½ cup of the sugar in a heavy 8-inch skillet (cast iron is best for this or heavy copper pot), stirring constantly, until the sugar is melted and golden brown. Remove from heat; stir in boiling water slowly. Cook over low heat, stirring constantly, until sugar lumps are dissolved. Add enough water to syrup, if necessary, to measure ½ cup; cool.

2. Beat egg whites in small mixing bowl until foamy. Beat in ½ cup of the sugar, 1 teaspoon at a time; continue beating until very stiff and glossy. Reserve meringue.

3. Sift together flour, baking powder, and salt.

4. Beat butter, remaining ½ cup of sugar, the egg yolks, and vanilla for 30 seconds on low speed in the larger mixing bowl, scraping bowl constantly. Beat for five minutes on high speed, scraping bowl occasionally. Beat in syrup. Add flour, baking powder, and salt alternately with milk. Fold in reserved meringue. Pour into prepared pans.

5. Bake until wooden toothpick inserted in center comes out clean, about 20 to 25 minutes. Cool for 10 minutes, remove from pans, and then let cool completely. Fill layers and frost cake with Caramel Frosting.

Caramel Frosting

This frosting tastes great on the Burnt Sugar Cake.

Ingredients:

2 tablespoons butter or margarine

⅔ cup packed dark brown sugar

⅛ teaspoon salt

⅓ cup whipping cream or evaporated milk

2 ⅓ to 2 ½ cups powdered sugar

½ teaspoon vanilla

1. Heat butter in two-quart saucepan until melted.

2. Stir in brown sugar, salt, and cream. Heat to boiling, stirring constantly.

3. Remove from heat; cool to lukewarm.

4. Stir in vanilla.

5. Gradually stir in powdered sugar until of spreading consistency.

Carrot Cake

This recipe makes four 7-inch layers or three 9-inch layers.

Ingredients:

2 cups sugar

1⅓ cups Crisco oil

4 unbeaten eggs

2 cups all purpose flour

2 teaspoons baking powder

2 teaspoons baking soda

2 teaspoons cinnamon

1 teaspoon salt

1 teaspoon vanilla

3 cups grated carrots (about 10–12 carrots)

½ cup pecan or walnut pieces (optional)

Needed:

1 large mixing bowl

1 small mixing bowl

Rubber spatula

Electric mixer

Sifter

Four 7" or three 9" cake pans

Parchment paper

Prep time: 10 minutes

Baking time: 20–25 minutes (375 degrees F)

Preheat oven to 375F. Set rack in middle of oven.

1. In large bowl sift together the flour, baking powder, soda, cinnamon, and salt.

2. In small bowl, add oil to sugar.

3. Add eggs to sugar/oil mixture.

4. Add egg/oil/sugar mixture to flour mixture and stir well.

5. Add grated carrots and stir.

6. Add vanilla.

7. Add nuts if you are using them.

8. Bake at 375 degrees for about 20–25 minutes or until a toothpick comes out clean.

Cream Cheese Frosting

This is a basic cream cheese frosting: buttercream with cream cheese substituted for part of the butter. It's okay to use neufchatel in this recipe if you want to reduce some of the fat content.

Ingredients:

8 ounces regular cream cheese (the kind that comes in a brick)

½ stick butter or margarine

2 teaspoons vanilla

1 box powdered sugar

1. Cream butter, cream cheese, and vanilla together.

2. Add sugar slowly. Beat until of spreading consistency.

Tawny Torte

This is the recipe Linda uses in her bakery every day. It makes an excellent chocolate cake, light, yet dark and chocolate-y. You'll love it!

Ingredients:

6 oz. Lindt or Ghirardelli milk chocolate

½ cup boiling water

1 cup softened (room temperature) butter

1½ cup granulated sugar

1 cup buttermilk

4 eggs

1 tsp vanilla

2½ cups sifted cake flour

1 tsp soda

½ tsp salt

Needed:

1 small saucepan

1 large mixing bowl

2 small mixing bowls

Rubber spatula

Electric mixer

Sifter

Two 8" or 9" round pans

Parchment paper

Prep time: 20–25 minutes

Baking time: 35 minutes (350 degrees F)

Preheat oven to 350F. Set rack in middle of oven. Grease and flour pans and line with parchment paper.

1. Melt chocolate in boiling water.

2. Cream together butter and sugar.

3. Add to creamed mixture four egg yolks, one at a time. Add vanilla.

4. Fold the chocolate and butter/sugar mixtures together.

5. Sift together flour, soda, and salt.

6. Add dry ingredients, alternately with buttermilk, to the creamed mixture.

7. Whip four egg whites to stiff peaks.

8. Fold into the batter.

9. Bake at 350 degrees in the 8" or 9" greased and floured pans for 30–35 minutes.

No Fail Chocolate Ganache

This ganache is just too easy to make, and it is useful as a sauce to serve over ice cream or with any other cake or dessert.

Ingredients:

2 pounds Nestle's miniature morsels (do not substitute)

2 cups half and half

¼ cup sugar

1. Heat half and half and sugar in double boiler over medium heat until steam starts.

2. Pour over mini morsels.

3. Stir until smooth. Refrigerate any unused portions for up to two weeks.

Waldorf-Astoria Red Velvet Cake

We have seen many versions of this recipe, but none matches this one for a moist, tasty, delicious, and absolutely not-to-be-matched-anywhere beautiful red cake. It's appropriate for holiday meals, birthdays, and all special occasions.

Ingredients:

⅔ cup shortening

1½ cup sugar

2 eggs

1 tablespoon cocoa (Hershey's is best for this.)

1 ounce (one full bottle) red food coloring

1 ounce water (measure in empty food coloring bottle)

1½ cup all purpose flour

1 teaspoon salt

1 cup buttermilk

1 teaspoon vanilla

1 tablespoon vinegar

1 teaspoon soda

Needed:

1 large mixing bowl

2 small mixing bowls

Rubber spatula

Electric mixer

Sifter

Two 9" round pans

Parchment paper

Prep time: 15–20 minutes

Baking time: 35 minutes (350 degrees F)

Preheat oven to 350F. Set rack in middle of oven. Grease, flour, and line with parchment paper two 9" pans.

1. Cream the shortening and sugar until fluffy.

2. Add one egg at a time and beat well after each addition.

3. Make a paste of cocoa, food coloring, and water and add to creamed mixture.

4. Sift together the salt and flour and add to creamed mixture, alternating with buttermilk and beginning and ending with flour.

5. Add vanilla.

6. Mix soda and vinegar and add to mixture.

7. Do not beat at this stage, but fold gently until blended.

8. Bake at 350 degrees for about 35 minutes.

Cool the cake completely. Then split layers of cake, stack, and frost between and on top and sides with Waldorf-Astoria Frosting.

Waldorf-Astoria Frosting

Ingredients:

⅔ cup Gold Medal Wondra flour

1 cup milk

1 teaspoon vanilla

1 cup sugar

1 cup margarine or butter

1. Mix instant flour with cold milk. Cook flour and milk together until thick, stirring constantly with a whisk. (Double boiler is best.)

2. Cool.

3. Cream butter and sugar until light and fluffy.

4. Add a little of the creamed butter and sugar (two tablespoons) to the cooled flour/milk mixture.

5. Put everything back in the butter/sugar mixture in small mixing bowl and beat until fluffy.

6. Add vanilla.

Silver Cake

Silver cake is like white cake only more so—a bit lighter, sweeter, and with a finer crumb. Delicious!

Ingredients:

3 cups sifted cake flour

3 teaspoons baking powder

½ teaspoon salt

⅔ cup shortening

2 cups sugar

1 teaspoon vanilla

1 cup milk

5 egg whites

Needed:

1 large mixing bowl

2 small mixing bowls

Rubber spatula

Electric mixer

Sifter

Three 9" round pans

Parchment paper

Prep time: 15 minutes

Baking time: 30 minutes (350 degrees F)

Preheat oven to 350F. Set rack in middle of oven. Grease, flour, and line with parchment paper the pans.

1. Sift flour, baking powder, and salt together in small mixing bowl.

2. In large bowl, cream shortening with sugar and vanilla until fluffy.

3. Add sifted dry ingredients and milk alternately in small amounts, beating well after each addition.

4. Beat egg whites until stiff but not dry and fold them into the batter.

5. Pour into greased pans and bake in moderate oven (350 degrees F) for 30 minutes.

Makes three 9-inch layers. Frost with buttercream frosting or fondant.

Golden Chiffon Cake

This is a light cake similar to sponge cake. It is most commonly used for petits fours. Chiffon batter should be baked immediately after blending. After baking, the cake should have a slightly coarse texture.

Ingredients:

2 ¼ cups sifted cake flour

1 ½ cups sugar

3 teaspoons baking powder

1 teaspoon salt

½ cup vegetable oil

5 egg yolks

3/4 cup water

1 teaspoon vanilla

½ teaspoon cream of tartar

1 cup egg whites (approximately 8)

Needed:

2 large mixing bowls

Electric mixer with whip

Sheet pan for petits fours

Or springform pan for Boston cream pie

Parchment paper

Prep time: 10–15 minutes

Baking time: (325 degrees F)
    for sheet pan 10–15 minutes
    springform pan 30-35 minutes

Preheat oven to 325F. Set rack in middle of oven. Grease and flour and line with parchment paper the baking pans.

1. Sift together cake flour, sugar, baking powder, and salt in the center of a large mixing bowl.

2. Add oil, egg yolks, water, and vanilla (a little at a time). Mix until satin smooth.

3. Combine egg whites and cream of tartar in a separate mixing bowl.

4. Beat with whip attachment until very stiff peaks form.

5. Gently fold the two mixtures together.

6. Gently pour final mixture into parchment lined pans and bake as directed above.

See the instructions in Chapter 4 for Petits Fours and Boston cream pie.

More Frostings and Fillings

Buttercream Frosting

This is how the commercial bakeries make it. The butter provides flavor, the shortening provides a more neutral color and smooth consistency. The recipe shown here makes a big batch of frosting (enough for two stacked cakes), but it can be easily cut in half if you just want to make a small amount to crumb coat a cake before you add another type of frosting. This frosting works as a finish for any recipe in this book, or it is useful as a crumb coating before you enrobe a cake in fondant.

Ingredients:

1 pound butter

1 pound Crisco

2 pounds sugar

2 teaspoons vanilla flavoring

Cream together the butter and shortening. Add sugar gradually until it is blended throughout. You may vary the flavor by replacing one teaspoon of the vanilla with almond extract or by adding three tablespoons of cocoa.

For cream cheese frosting, add 8 ounces of cream cheese to the butter/Crisco mixture. Then increase the sugar by about ½ cup.

Chocolate Mousse

This is great as a filling for the tawny torte, the golden chiffon cake, or the chocolate torte recipe on page 58. It's also great just to serve as chocolate mousse with a dollop of whipped cream. A tablespoon or two of Amaretto or raspberry-flavored liqueur gives it a more sophisticated taste.

Ingredients:

11 ounces of Lindt, Ghirardelli, or a really good semi-sweet chocolate

¾ cup cold butter

5 egg yolks

8 egg whites

3 ½ tablespoons sugar

1. Melt the chocolate over a double boiler. Cool to room temperature. Stir in cold butter in small pats to cool the chocolate.

2. Add egg yolks and stir. Do not whip at this point.

3. Whip the egg whites to a medium peak. Add sugar and continue to beat until very firm.

4. Fold the two mixtures together with long folding strokes.

5. Cool to room temperature and refrigerate overnight.

Raspberry Sauce

Ingredients:

2 cups fresh or frozen raspberries

½ cup sugar

Lemon juice

Clean fresh raspberries or allow frozen ones to thaw in a strainer over a bowl. Cook the berries and sugar together until it all forms a sauce and thickens. Add a squeeze of lemon juice. Serve with any cake or spoon over ice cream.

Lemon Curd

Perfect for petits fours fillings.

Ingredients:

2 cups butter

2 cups lemon juice

5 cups sugar

12 eggs

Boil butter and lemon juice together. Add sugar and eggs. Makes one quart. You can keep this for up to two weeks in the refrigerator. It's great as just a dipping sauce for sugar cookies. You can also mix it half and half with whipped cream for a light, frothy lemon mousse-type dessert.

Crème Fraiche Substitute

Crème fraiche is a rich, nutty-tasting topping made from unpasteurized cream that has been allowed to ferment. It's a specialty in France, but is not sold here because using unpasteurized milk or cream is not allowed in the United States. It's wonderful atop the chocolate torte on page 58 topped with ganache. Here's a simple way to make your own.

Ingredients:

1 cup heavy cream

2 tablespoons buttermilk

Allow to stand at room temperature for 8 to 24 hours until it thickens.
Stir and refrigerate for up to 10 days.

Pastry Cream

This is the filling for the Boston Cream Pie pictured later in the book. It's also used to fill Bismarks, cream horns, and all sorts of pastries.

Ingredients:

1 quart milk

1 cup sugar

3 teaspoons cornstarch

3 eggs

1 pat butter

1 tablespoon vanilla

1. Bring milk just to a boil in medium saucepan.

2. Meanwhile, mix sugar and cornstarch in a small mixing bowl.

3. Add eggs to sugar and cornstarch.

4. Add butter and vanilla and mix well.

5. Put a little of the milk (about ¼ cup) in the sugar/cornstarch/egg mixture.

6. Put everything back into the pot with the rest of the milk and bring to a boil once more.

Store in airtight container up to one week.

Royal Icing for Decorating

This is the stuff we use to make those little butterflies on the tea cakes and the violets on the violet cake in Chapter 5. It sets up hard and colors well and is perfect when you want something decorative that will hold its shape. You wouldn't frost a cake with this; it's just for molding and making decorative items like flowers to brighten up your frosted cake.

Ingredients:

3 egg whites

6 cups powdered sugar

1 teaspoon cream of tartar

1 teaspoon lemon juice

Beat egg whites. Add cream of tartar, sugar, and lemon juice and continue beating to stiff peak stage. Immediately cover with plastic wrap to keep from hardening until you are ready to use it. Use gel food coloring, available in grocery and craft stores (or Americolor Gel food coloring from Sweet Art, Inc.), to attain just the color you want, from pastel to the most vivid shades imaginable.

Bonus Recipes

THE FOLLOWING RECIPES AREN'T used for the decorated cakes in this book. They are, however, very good, and we wanted to share with you a couple of cakes we like to whip up when our kids call and say "What's for dinner?" You can quickly make these cakes while the roast is in the oven. These are good everyday recipes for cakes our families love.

Chocolate Cake

Ingredients:

1 ½ cups sugar

2 cups all purpose flour

1 stick margarine

1 teaspoon salt

1 teaspoon soda

1 cup buttermilk—mix soda with buttermilk

1 teaspoon vanilla

3 tablespoons Hershey's cocoa

1 egg + ¼ cup water

Needed:

1 large mixing bowl

1 small mixing bowl

Rubber spatula

Electric mixer

Sifter

13 × 9" cake pan

Prep time: 10 minutes

Baking time: 30 minutes (350 degrees F)

Preheat oven to 350F. Set rack in middle of oven. Grease and flour baking pan. Do not line with parchment.

1. Sift together flour, salt, and cocoa.

2. Cream sugar and butter. Add egg and water. Add vanilla.

3. Add flour mixture to sugar/butter/egg mixture, alternating with buttermilk, beginning and ending with flour.

4. Bake for 25 to 30 minutes

5. Cool for half an hour and then pour icing over cake in pan. Icing will be shiny. This is divine if you make one batch, pour it over the cake, let it cool, and then make another batch and pour it over the first one.

Oatmeal Cake

Ingredients:

1 cup oats

1 ½ cups boiling water

1 stick butter

Pour water over oats and butter; let stand 20 minutes.

Then add:

1 cup brown sugar

1 cup white sugar

2 eggs

1 teaspoon vanilla

Sift together the following ingredients and add them to the mixture:

1 teaspoon soda

½ teaspoon salt

1 ½ cup flour

Stir well and bake in greased and floured pan for 30 to 35 minutes at 350 degrees. Do not line pan with parchment.

Needed:

1 large mixing bowl

1 small mixing bowl

Wooden spoon

13 × 9" cake pan

Prep time: 10 minutes

Baking time: 30 minutes (350 degrees F)

Chocolate Cake Icing

Ingredients:

1 cup sugar

Dash salt

1/3 cup milk

½ stick margarine

3 tablespoons Hershey's cocoa

1 teaspoon vanilla

Cook in small saucepan for about 10 minutes. Set the pan in a sink containing about two inches of cold water. Beat with spoon until of spreading consistency. Don't beat too long or this will turn into fudge. Pour on cooled cake.

Oatmeal Cake Icing

Ingredients:

1 cup brown sugar

½ cup milk

4 tablespoons butter

½ cup (or more) pecans

½ cup (or more) shredded or flaked coconut

Boil first three ingredients for five minutes. Add nuts and coconut. Spread on warm cake and set under broiler for a few minutes until it begins to bubble and brown. Watch closely to make sure it doesn't burn.

Chocolate Torte

Ingredients:

1 cup unsalted butter, cut into small pieces

9 ounces Lindt semisweet or bittersweet chocolate, cut into small pieces

6 large eggs, separated

1 cup granulated white sugar, divided

1 teaspoon pure vanilla extract

¼ teaspoon cream of tartar

Needed:

Double boiler

Two medium or large mixing bowls

Mixer

Springform pan

Prep time: 20 minutes

Baking time: 50–60 minutes
(350 degrees F)

Make this the day before so the flavors have time to meld together.

1. Preheat oven to 350. Place rack in middle position in oven. Coat a 9" × 3" springform pan with butter or cooking spray and line with parchment. Coat parchment with butter or cooking spray.

2. Separate cold eggs. Cover each egg part with plastic wrap and let them warm to room temperature.

3. Melt the butter and chocolate together in a stainless steel double boiler.

4. Place egg yolks and ½ cup sugar in mixing bowl and beat at medium high speed for about five minutes using paddle attachment if you have one, until lemon-colored and smooth. Eggs should triple in volume, and when you lift the mixer, the mixture should form a thin ribbon as it falls back into the bowl.

5. Add vanilla and chocolate mixture to egg yolks.

6. In a separate bowl, beat egg whites until foamy. Add cream of tartar and continue beating until soft peaks form. Gradually add ½ cup sugar and continue beating until stiff peaks form.

7. Fold a small amount of the egg whites into the egg yolk mixture. Continue adding egg whites and folding into the egg yolk mixture until it is all incorporated. Do not overmix. Fold gently.

8. Pour carefully into the prepared springform pan, smoothing the top.

9. Bake in preheated 350-degree oven for 50 to 60 minutes, until a toothpick inserted in the middle comes out clean or with just a few dry crumbs.

10. Remove from oven and allow to cool in pan for a few minutes. At this point, the hard crust that formed will "fall," and the cake will have an uneven surface with lots of crumbs in evidence.

11. Turn upside down on serving platter or dish, remove the pan, and refrigerate for an hour.

12. Brush away any loose crumbs and apply a crumb coating of just a couple of tablespoons of ganache to lay the crumbs to rest. Refrigerate cake for five minutes to allow crumb coat to set. Then pour ganache into center of cake and work quickly to spread it to cover the entire cake.

Fondant Frosting

If you want to try making fondant frosting "from scratch," it's a very simple recipe, but time-consuming and hard work. Linda's Choco-Pan® fondant is what we used in Chapter 5 to create the cakes presented there, but you can also buy fondant from many suppliers, such as cake decorating shops and online suppliers. Or you can use this recipe to make it yourself.

Don't confuse fondant frosting with rolled fondant. Fondant frosting is poured over cakes and petits fours while warm. Rolled fondant is rolled out with a rolling pin and draped over cakes. Rolled fondant is the kind we show you how to work with in Chapter 5. It's a simple mixture of water, sugar, and cream of tartar that is cooked and then kneaded so that it becomes pliable.

Ingredients:

2 tablespoons unflavored gelatin

¼ cup cold water

½ cup glucose (available from cake decorating suppliers)

1 tablespoon glycerin (available from cake decorating suppliers)

2 tablespoons shortening

2 lbs. confectioner's sugar (add a dash of salt)

Gel food coloring

1 teaspoon vanilla flavoring (you can substitute almond, lemon, or any other extract)

Combine gelatin and cold water; let stand until thick. Place gelatin mixture in top of double boiler and heat until dissolved. Add glucose and mix well. Stir in shortening and just before the shortening is completely melted, remove the mixture from the heat. Add glycerin. Add flavoring and food coloring as desired. Cool until lukewarm. Next, place 4 cups confectioner's sugar in a bowl and make a well. Pour the lukewarm gelatin mixture into the well and stir with a wooden spoon, mixing in sugar and adding more, a little at a time, until stickiness disappears. Knead in remaining sugar. Knead until the fondant is smooth and pliable and does not stick to your hands. If the fondant is too soft, add more sugar; if too stiff, add water (a drop at a time). Use fondant immediately or store in airtight container in a cool, dry place. Do not refrigerate or freeze. When ready to use, knead again until soft.

Fondant, whether home-made or purchased already made, gives your cakes a sculpture-like finish.
Here are a few of the things Linda will teach you to make with fondant later in the book and on the DVD.

4

Simple Decorating Techniques

In Chapter 3, we shared with you some of the absolute best cake recipes available. Now we'd like to show you some simple presentations (and some not-so-simple ones) that you can use to create, not just the best tasting desserts around, but also the best looking. The creations we present here are ones that any beginner can accomplish with practice. They are simple, yet beautiful cakes that we know will cause your family and guests to be amazed at your creativity and skill. You don't have to be a chef to bake the cakes we showed you how to bake in Chapter 3, and you don't have to be an artist to follow the instructions here for decorating them.

This chapter contains step-by-step instructions for decorating your cakes with buttercream frosting and melted chocolate—easy to make ingredients that you can find locally. Occasionally, we'll suggest using ribbon, beads, and specially shaped pans, but these are all available at your nearest craft store.

Sunday Supper Caramel Cake

Bake the Burnt Sugar Cake on page 40 using two 9-inch round cake pans. Cool for five minutes in pans, then remove cake from pans and allow to cool completely on wire racks.

Make a double batch of the Caramel Frosting on page 41.

Make one batch of the No Fail Chocolate Ganache on page 45.

Place a dollop of frosting in the middle of the serving plate, spread it a bit, and then place the first layer on top. This helps secure the cake to the dish.

Spread a generous layer of frosting on top of the first layer and add the second layer.

Brush away any loose crumbs, and then spread a thin layer of frosting over the entire cake. This is the crumb coating, and it makes finishing the decorative layer of frosting much easier. After the cake is crumb coated, refrigerate it for at least one hour.

> To make your cake layers level, trim them while they are still in the pan. If you start with a level cake, your finished product will be that much more beautiful.
>
> To check whether a layer is level, lay your cake knife atop the sides of the pan and move it from side to side. If the middle of the cake layer has risen higher than the pan, just trim it off level with the sides of the pan. And there you have it! If each layer is level, the cake itself will be level.

When crumb coating, your spatula should never touch the bare cake so as not to disturb the surface and create more crumbs. Work quickly, spreading the frosting on smoothly, just thick enough to coat the entire cake. At this point, there's no need to try for decorative swirls or peaks.

Remove the cake from the refrigerator and place it on its serving dish on a rotating turntable if one is available. If not, you will just need to turn the cake by hand to accomplish the circular movement that results in the frosting method shown here.

Spread the final layer of frosting with a small offset spatula until it is evenly distributed over the entire cake.

Using a circular motion, go around the top edge of the cake with the spatula. Add more frosting as you need it.

When you have plenty of frosting on the top of the cake, start in the middle and work your way outward, creating a pinwheel design.

This is easy if you have a turntable. Just set the spatula in the center of the cake. Hold the spatula still and start swirling the cake on the stand. Let the frosting swirl naturally outward under the spatula.

To do the swirl effect on the sides, set your small spatula in one spot and, using a swirling motion, circle and lift the spatula as you reach the end of the circle. Keep doing this so that your swirls overlap and all sides of the cake are covered in little swirls.

Using a large pastry tube with no tip, apply ganache around the edges, allowing it to trickle over the sides. Serve plain.

To make this simple Sunday night supper cake really elegant, add heaps of mixed berries on top and allow them to cascade over the side. Dust with confectioner's sugar.

Easter Bunny Carrot Cake

MAKE ONE RECIPE OF THE CARROT cake on page 42 and two recipes of the cream cheese frosting on page 43. Bake the cake in a 9" × 13" cake pan at 375 F for 25–30 minutes or until a toothpick inserted in the center comes out clean, cool for five minutes in the pan, and then turn it onto a wire rack to cool completely. After it's cooled, place a serving dish or foil-covered board upside down on top of the cake and invert the whole thing.

Make the frosting and reserve two half cups; using gel food coloring, color one half cup orange and the other green. The shades can vary according to your taste; you don't have to match the shade we show here exactly.

You also need a couple of Oreo cookies, some melted chocolate for writing on the cake, a pastry tube with a #7 tip for the carrots and a #65 tip for the leaves, and a chocolate Easter bunny.

Brush away any loose crumbs and crumb coat the entire cake using the cream cheese frosting. Refrigerate for at least one hour.

After the cake has been refrigerated, cover the whole cake with a generous layer of cream cheese frosting, spreading it smoothly. To get a smooth frosting effect, work in one direction, smoothing the icing, then in the opposite direction, smoothing it more. Keep working back and forth until the frosting is smooth looking.

Expert tip from Linda

Using a pastry tube is something that is only mastered with time. The first time you try this, you probably won't be completely satisfied with the results. Keep practicing. Cake decorating is like learning a musical instrument. Practice makes perfect. In this case though, the results are always edible.

Fill a pastry tube with white frosting and make a decorative shell border along the top edge of cake and around the bottom of cake.

For the bottom, use a pastry bag with shell tip #32 (an open star tip). Place the tip against the base of the cake at a 45 degree angle. Apply gentle pressure to the tube and allow a "puff" of frosting to build to the desired size. Stop pressure and then pull the tip away from the surface of the cake. Place the tip at the end of that shell and repeat the motion, all the way around the cake. Strive for consistency. Your shells may not be exactly like the ones shown in the pictures here, but they'll look good if they are all pretty much the same size. Consistency is the first step toward perfection.

For the top edge, use pastry tube #32 again. Repeat the same motion you did for the bottom border, drawing each application out a bit longer this time to create more of a shell shape instead of the puffs of frosting on the bottom border.

Expert tip from Linda

The consistency of your icing will make a difference in how much pressure you need to apply, how much icing you'll use, and how the final product will appear. Follow the directions for the frosting recipes, but humidity and heat can affect spreadability and how the frosting comes through the pastry tube. You need to be flexible and ready to add more sugar or more shortening to your frosting mixture. The more you work with spreading frosting and using a pastry tube, the more you'll be familiar with how it should look and feel—and the more skilled and confident you'll become.

Separate the Oreo cookies and scrape off the filling. Crush the cookies and sprinkle in one corner to make "dirt" for the carrot patch.

Fill a pastry tube with the orange icing and, using tip #07, make the carrots. Hold the tip close to the cake at a 45 degree angle and apply pressure to force the frosting through the tip. As the icing appears, begin making small circular motions, coiling the icing into the shape of a carrot. Continue coiling the icing, maintaining a gentle pressure on the tube to make whole carrots lying on the ground. As you reach the end of the carrot, lessen the pressure and pull the tip away from the cake. This will make the carrot appear to have a pointed end.

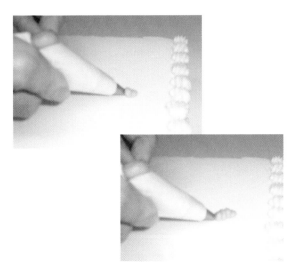

Make a few of these in the Oreo dirt and a few off to the side. You can also just make a small squirt of frosting in the dirt for carrots that are peeking through but haven't been pulled yet. Add their green tops when you start working with the green frosting.Put a few carrots around the edges of the cake in the border too.

Next, fill a pastry tube with green icing and with tip #65 (leaf tip) make the carrot tops. Just apply slight pressure and pull off into a point.

Place the chocolate bunny in an empty corner. (It's better if you can find a bunny holding a carrot.)

Use the pastry tube filled with melted chocolate to write Happy Easter on the bottom half of the cake. You can just use a small hand-made parchment pastry tube for this with the end snipped off. (See the pastry tube instructions on page 29.)

Use any good chocolate to melt for this or any writing project. Just heat it to 98 to 100 degrees F. and fill the pastry tube with it.

Squeeze out some icing from the pastry tube to get it going good before you start to decorate with a tube to release trapped air.

Picnic with Boston Cream Pie

FOR THIS CLASSIC CAKE you will need one recipe of Golden Chiffon Cake on page 49, one recipe of Pastry Cream on page 53, and one recipe of No Fail Chocolate Ganache on page 45.

Grease and flour the bottom and sides of a springform pan. Line the bottom of the pan with parchment paper and grease and flour it as well.

Bake the Golden Chiffon Cake recipe in the parchment-lined springform pan for 30–35 minutes, or until a toothpick inserted in the center comes out clean and the cake pulls away from the sides of the pan.

Allow the cake to cool in the pan for a few minutes, and then release the spring and remove the sides from pan.

Lift the pan sides off the cake.

Use a knife, if necessary, to loosen the cake from the pan bottom, and gently remove cake with parchment paper from the bottom of pan.

Peel the parchment gently from the cake.

Place a serving plate on the turntable and then place the cake on the plate.

Use the cake (*torting*) knife to split the cake into two layers.

Hold a knife level and turn the turntable to score the sides of the cake (or just turn the cake with your hands if you don't have a turntable). When you split the layers, use the scoring as a guideline to keep the knife level. After the cake is marked, you can cut it easily.

Split the scored cake and place the top half to the side.

Spread the pastry cream thickly on the cake.

Allow the pastry cream to slightly cool and then apply a generous amount to the bottom half of the split cake.

Place the top half of the split cake gently back on top of pastry cream covered bottom.

Using a small cup to pour from, top the cake with ganache. Turn the cake slowly and pour ganache gently around the edges.

Allow it to slightly drip over the side, forming a delicious chocolate drizzle.

Fill in the center with chocolate ganache.

Use a large offset spatula to spread the ganache on top.

Red Velvet Cake for Christmas

OF COURSE, THIS CAKE DOESN'T have to be reserved just for Christmas, but no Christmas dinner would be complete without it. It's the cake many of our family members also request for their birthdays or other special occasions.

Make the Waldorf-Astoria Red Velvet Cake recipe on page 46, baking the cake in two 9-inch round cake pans, greased and floured and lined with parchment paper.

Make a double batch of the special Waldorf-Astoria Frosting on page 47.

Let the cake completely cool. Split the layers using a long serrated cake (or torting) knife, and make sure to reserve a few of the resulting crumbs for decorating the finished product. Take your time when splitting the layers, stopping occasionally to make sure your knife is still level. Use the scoring method described in the instructions for Boston Cream Pie.

Real life tip from Sandy

Red velvet cake is the pièce de résistance of all our family gatherings. My mother is famous for this cake, and as soon as the idea of a cake decorating book was proposed to me, I knew this recipe had to be in it. It's known among our family and friends as, simply, "red cake," but it's unlike any other red cake you'll ever be served. It is a true gem, and it is different from any other red velvet cake recipe I have seen.

I think that may be because this might just be the original recipe, unimproved upon as cooks passed it from one to another and as typos slipped in or someone thought they could improve upon it in some way. Where did this recipe originate? The story goes that a couple on vacation in New York City had dinner at the Waldorf-Astoria dining room. The woman praised the beautiful red cake that was served to her and asked that her compliments be conveyed to the chef. She also asked for the recipe for the cake. The waiter said that if she would give him her address, the chef would be happy to send her a copy of the recipe. She gratefully complied. A few weeks later, the recipe arrived in the mail along with an invoice for $200. Angered by the unexpected charge, the woman set about to share the recipe with as many people as possible.

That story has been around a long time and may or may not be true, but this recipe fell into my mother's hands, along with the story, about 50 years ago. She set about to make the cake and quickly became somewhat famous for it, perhaps because she was one of the few people who could make the frosting turn out right. Her recipe, the one she still uses today, is on page 46. When I did the research for this book, I searched for red velvet cake recipes, red cake recipes, and Waldorf-Astoria cake recipes online and in every cookbook I could find. Not one exactly matched the one my mother uses; generally, they all include an extra cup of flour. Most recipes just say to use cream cheese frosting for this cake. My mother's recipe calls for the modified buttercream frosting recipe on page 47. Over the years, she did modify the frosting recipe to use granulated sugar when castor or superfine sugar became too difficult to find. She also changed it when Gold Medal Wondra instant flour became available. She uses that in the frosting now because it's less likely to lump. Here's a secret: Add a squirt of lemon juice to help "cut" the grain of the sugar and make the frosting even more smooth. Cake and frosting together—I have not found their match anywhere.

Expert tip from Linda

Insert a cardboard round or a flat plate between the layers and slide the top half onto a flat surface. Repeat with the second layer, so that you have four thin layers of cake. You can use a round of cardboard, a plate, a cookie sheet that doesn't have a "lip," or a pizza stone. All you need is a flat, inflexible surface.

Fill the cake with Waldorf-Astoria frosting. Stack all four layers, spreading the filling generously between each layer.

Crumb coat the entire cake and refrigerate for at least an hour.

Frost the cake using swirling motions with an offset spatula. Cover the top and sides with a generous layer of swirled icing.

Use the reserved crumbs to sprinkle some color in the center of the finished cake. Finish with a sprinkle of red sugar crystals around the top edge of the cake. Serve on your best china.

Groom's Cake

GROOM'S CAKE IS A TRADITION in some parts of the country. In the past this has been a dense, heavy cake, often a fruit cake or rum cake. It was often served in individual take-home serving-sized boxes, one for each guest. The idea was if a single woman put a piece of this cake under her pillow, she'd dream of her own groom. The idea has morphed over the decades into the current idea of making a cake that reflects the interests of the groom. Groom's cakes are usually chocolate or perhaps a pound cake—a foil for the delicate white confection that is the wedding cake.

Red velvet cake in the shape of an armadillo was famously used for the groom's cake in the movie *Steel Magnolias*. Here, however, we use the Tawny Torte recipe from Chapter 3 with No Fail Chocolate Ganache and those cute little strawberry tuxedos, representative of the groom and his groomsmen.

Bake one recipe of Tawny Torte on page 44. Use two 9-inch round cake pans, and bake as directed. Cool five minutes, then remove from pans and allow to cool on wire racks to room temperature.

Make one recipe of chocolate ganache and one recipe of buttercream frosting. Divide the buttercream frosting in half, flavoring one half with vanilla and one half with chocolate. (Just sift a little dry cocoa powder with the sugar before you blend it with the butter.)

You will also need a tub of melted dark chocolate and a tub of melted white chocolate, and two pastry tubes with a very small snip taken off the end.

We recommend pâte à glacer, available from Sweet Art Galleries, for the melted chocolate. (See the ordering information at the back of the book.) You can also find fine melting chocolate at any gourmet culinary store, such as Williams-Sonoma.

Split the layers following the instructions in the Boston Cream Pie and Red Velvet Cake sections.

Stack and fill the layers with the vanilla flavored butter cream frosting. Use the chocolate buttercream frosting to crumb coat the cake. Place the cake in the refrigerator for about an hour to allow the crumb coat to set. Remove the cake and apply the ganache. Pour it in the middle and work quickly to spread it to the edges and cover the sides of the entire cake. Smooth the sides with an offset spatula, working first from side to side, then up and down, until the sides are well coated and smooth.

Use a pastry tube filled with melted white chocolate to pipe four circles on the top of the cake. Then use a straight edge knife to draw eight lines from the center to the edge of the cake, creating a feathered appearance to the white chocolate.

To make the strawberry tuxedos:
Wash and pat dry about two dozen large red strawberries. Get the best looking ones you can find.

Fill one deep cup or soup bowl with melted white chocolate and one with melted dark chocolate. Make sure the bowl you use is deep enough to dip the strawberries without letting them touch the bottom.

Line a cookie sheet with parchment paper.

Pick up a strawberry by its stem and dip it straight into the white chocolate. Leave a small rim of red showing at the top. Hold it over the bowl until it stops dripping; then place it on the parchment paper.

Continue working until you have dipped all the strawberries in white chocolate. Allow the chocolate to harden.

Pick up each strawberry again and, this time holding it at an angle, dip in the dark chocolate. Place on parchment to harden again.

Continue dipping until you have finished all the strawberries. Then, repeat the process with the dark chocolate, this time holding at an angle in the opposite direction, to create a V-shaped triangle of white at the top of each chocolate dipped berry. You must dip each strawberry twice in the dark chocolate, holding them at opposite facing angles in order to achieve the V-shape of the tuxedo. Again, hold the berry over the cup until it stops dripping and then place on parchment paper to dry.

Let all the strawberries harden and dry for a few minutes. Then cut them away from the parchment paper using a small offset spatula.

Fill a small pastry tube with melted dark chocolate. Cut a very small opening in the end and squeeze out a small amount of chocolate onto the parchment paper to remove air and start the chocolate flowing.

Pipe two chocolate buttons onto the white "shirt" in the V of the dark chocolate.

Use chocolate butter cream frosting to affix the strawberries around the bottom edge of the cake. Put two or three on top as a finishing touch.

Pipe on the outline of a bow tie at the top of the white chocolate and fill the outline with chocolate. Let the strawberries harden and dry on parchment paper.

THIS IS A TEENAGE GIRLS' CAKE, one for special teenage birthdays and coming of age celebrations—the bat mitzvah, quinceañera, or sweet 16. It could be adapted for any girl's birthday or even for a small wedding or anniversary celebration. The combing technique you'll learn here works on any cake with buttercream frosting. We chose to make this a burnt sugar cake with pink and white buttercream, but you could use any color for the foundation frosting layer and any flavor cake. The silver cake recipe on page 48 is also a good choice for this "sweetheart" cake. Because it's a tiered cake, you could even do two different flavors.

For this cake you will need two 8-inch heart-shaped cake pans and one 6-inch heart-shaped cake pan. These are available in cake decorating and craft stores everywhere. You will also need four dowel rods and a dowel rod cutter—these two items are available in all cake decorating and craft stores. You can find them at Michael's and at Wal-Mart, among other places. You will need two batches of buttercream frosting: one colored pale pink and one left white.

Make one recipe of the burnt sugar or silver cake and bake it in parchment-lined pans according to the directions in Chapter 3. (It's especially important that you grease and flour the heart-shaped pans well and use parchment paper because it can be more tricky getting the cake out of these pans.)

Allow the layers to cool. Stack and fill the 8-inch layers with any filling you want: buttercream frosting, raspberry filling, lemon curd, or any of the fillings and frostings in Chapter 3. Apply a crumb coating to the first tier of your cake.

The next step is to carefully center the dowel rods beneath where the 6-inch cake will be placed. Use the 6-inch pan to establish placement. Just turn it upside down and center it on the cake. When you are sure you have the placement right, press lightly to mark the crumb coated cake with the outline of the 6-inch pan.

Insert the dowel rods into the cake about three inches apart, centered around the outline of the 6-inch pan. Make sure they are evenly spaced to provide balanced support. Press firmly so that they reach all the way to the bottom of the cake and come to rest on the serving dish. If they stick out above the cake, you'll need to trim them off so that they are level with the cake. Use the dowel rod cutter to do this.

Then reinsert them into the cake in their already marked places.

Next carefully center the 6-inch layer atop the 8-inch cake.

Crumb coat the 6-inch cake and refrigerate the whole cake for at least an hour.

Remove the cake from the refrigerator and smooth coat the entire cake with the pink buttercream frosting. Place the cake in the freezer at this point and let it freeze—at least four hours—so that the pink frosting is hard.

Remove the cake from the freezer and use a large offset spatula to smooth coat it with a layer of white frosting.

Cover the entire cake smoothly and evenly with white frosting.

The next step is to comb the icing. The icing comb we use here is available at Sweet Art Galleries (www.choco-pan.com). You can also find these at craft stores and culinary stores everywhere. Michael's, Williams-Sonoma, and Sur la Table all carry icing combs.

Pull the comb firmly through the white icing, letting the underneath layer of pink shine through the white.

Turn and smooth several times, making sure the comb stays in the same track, and keeping the comb perpendicular to the cake.

Using a star tube or #30 tip, pipe on the border of white butter cream frosting.

To make the border, place the tube against the cake, squeeze, build up icing until it's the size you want, stop pressure, and pull the tube away. Repeat all the way around the edge of the cake.

Place a border around the top edge of the 6-inch tier, around the top edge of the 8-inch tier, and place first a white and then a pink border around the bottom of the 8-inch tier. You can use either white or pale pink icing for each of these borders. Vary them in any way that appeals to you. Follow the instructions in the Bunny Cake section for using the pastry tube to apply the borders.

We finished our cake with strings of 6 mm pearls, available at craft stores, and a couple pink carnations. The babies breath around the base of the cake stand adds a touch of romance and innocence to the presentation.

Petits Fours

MAKING PETITS FOURS SEEMS like quite a challenge—they're so small, so individual looking. It's as if someone baked dozens of tiny separate cakes, carefully stacking each layer with a tasty filling surprise and then covering each one in icing. The method we'll share with you here is one Linda uses in her bakery to turn out hundreds of these tiny, tasty little cakes, and it works wonders! It's easy to make these little cakes, and here Linda shares with you her professional secrets for turning them out quickly and beautifully every time.

For the petits fours you should use the Golden Chiffon Cake on page 49. You'll also need a filling. We chose Lemon Curd for ours, but you might also use the Raspberry Filling or the Chocolate Mousse recipes in Chapter 3. And you'll need some dipping chocolate: both white and milk chocolate. We recommend the pâte à glacer available for order at Sweet Art Galleries, but you can also find this at all fine culinary stores. You'll also need half a recipe of buttercream frosting (divided and colored, half yellow and half green) for the piped on flowers.

You'll need a couple of pastry tubes to pipe on the finishing touches. For dipping the petits fours, you'll need a wooden skewer and a plastic fork.

Bake the Golden Chiffon Cake in a greased, floured, and parchment-lined cookie sheet. Allow the cake to cool to room temperature, remove it from the pan, remove the parchment paper, and refrigerate the cake for a few hours.

Remove the cake from the refrigerator and, using a long torting knife, split the cake into two thin layers. Place the bottom half in a cookie sheet with a lip, fill with the lemon curd, and then place the top layer back on top.

At this point, you need to place some pressure on the cake to help meld the layers together. You also need to freeze it solid so that it's easier to cut and work with. On top of the stacked cake, place a second cookie sheet, right side up. Put a couple of paperback books or lightweight hardback books on top of the second cookie sheet and place the whole thing in the freezer overnight.

The following day, make sure all your equipment is ready and have your tubs of chocolate ready to coat the cakes after they are cut. When you're ready to begin making the petits fours turn the whole cake out onto a flat surface. Using a ruler, trim the edges from the cake to create a straight line on all sides. (You can throw these away, but please...don't. They make good snacks for all the people gathered around waiting for the petits fours to be finished.)

Then, using the ruler, measure and cut tiny 1" × 1" cakes.

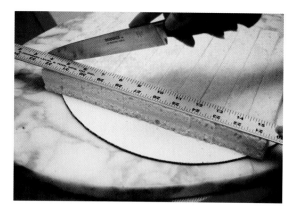

To dip the cakes in the chocolate and to remove them so that the chocolate can harden unblemished, you'll need a wooden skewer and a plastic fork with one tine broken out of it.

You'll also need two tubs of dipping chocolate: one white, one milk chocolate.

You want to work quickly at this point because the cakes will be easier to work with if they stay frozen. If necessary, return them to the freezer for an hour while you prepare the chocolate for dipping.

Using the skewer, spear one cake and dip it in the chocolate. (Do about half white chocolate and half milk chocolate, or any combination you prefer.)

Dip the cake completely in the chocolate.

Remove and hold the cake over the cup until it stops dripping.

Carefully remove the cake from the skewer, using the plastic fork to hold the cake. Fit the skewer into the opening left by the broken out tine of the fork, and carefully remove the skewer, leaving the cake sitting on the fork.

Use the fork to transfer the cake to a parchment-lined cookie sheet. Carefully slide the fork from beneath the cake, using the skewer to steady the cake.

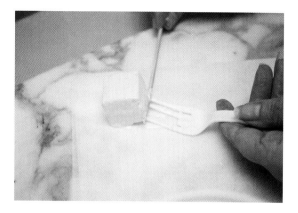

Continue dipping and placing the cakes on the cookie sheet until they are all covered in chocolate.

To decorate with fine lines:

Fill a small pastry bag with a contrasting color of chocolate—milk chocolate for the white coated pastries, and white chocolate for the dark coated pastries. Cut a tiny snip in the bottom of the bag and work quickly, moving back and forth, keeping a steady pressure on the pastry bag.

For the buttercream frosting decorations:

Fill a pastry bag with yellow (or any color you want) butter cream frosting. Using a #103 tip, pipe small flowers onto each cake.

Fill a second pastry bag with green butter cream frosting, use leaf tip #65, and pipe on the leaves.

Use a knife to trim away the excess chocolate and remove the cakes to a serving plate.

We used small candy papers to serve our cakes—it helps avoid sticky fingers!

In this chapter you learned some simple techniques for creating cakes from the simple to the simply sublime. In the next chapter, we take you one step further along the way to being a Sweet Artist. In Chapter 5, you'll learn tricks for working with royal icing, and you'll learn how to use fondant. You'll also learn more about some special tools available to make your baking and decorating look just like the professionals.

Serve these delicate pastries with a pot of tea on your finest china.
Your guests will be impressed by your culinary skills.

5

Decorating Cakes Using Fondant and Royal Icing

In Chapter 4, you learned how to work with buttercream and melted chocolate to create some cakes that are just as appealing and professional-looking as any you'll see in a bakery window. You learned how easy it is to go step-by-step to bake and decorate these cakes yourself and make them even better than any bakery can because you include that extra ingredient—love—that can only be found at home in your own kitchen.

Now we'll move on to some cakes that are just as easy to make and decorate but that require special ingredients, tools, or techniques to make. These are still completely within the reach of the amateur, and with the right ingredients and tools and just a little practice, you can make these great-looking cakes too. Remember, get out your best linens and lace tablecloths, polish the silver, and make a presentation out of each cake you put so much care and love into.

Baby Shower Cake

W E SUGGEST YOU USE THE Silver Cake recipe on page 48 for this cake, but if you prefer a different flavor, any of the recipes in Chapter 3 will work. Bake the cake in a 13" × 9" inch pan and cool it slightly in the pan. Then turn it onto a wire rack to finish cooling. After a couple of hours, turn the serving plate or foil-covered board you'll be using upside down over the cake, and invert the whole thing, cake, wire rack, and serving platter, so that the cake is resting on the serving dish. Gently remove the wire rack.

Make two recipes of buttercream or cream cheese frosting. Color two small portions (about half a cup) in any color combination you like. Pastel pink and green are used here for the roses and rose leaves.

You will also need a small piece of fondant for the blanket (about ¼ pound) in any color desired. (We chose pink for the fondant here too, but you could also use lavender, blue, or pale yellow.) Color the fondant using Americolor Gel paste food coloring, available from Sweet Art Galleries. Choco-Pan fondant is what we use here, and it too is available at Sweet Art Galleries. You will also need a small satin bow for the booties.

Crumb coat the cake and refrigerate it for a couple of hours. Add the final layer of buttercream frosting and smooth finish it with an offset spatula by smoothing it first in one direction and then in the other until the entire surface is smoothly frosted.

Using a pastry tube filled with white buttercream frosting and shell tip #32 or larger, make a border around the edge of the cake, following the directions in Chapter 4 for the Easter Bunny Carrot Cake.

Using a pastry tube filled with pink frosting and #14 tip, make smaller piped border about an inch inside the edge of the cake.

Use pink icing and #32 tip to pipe a finishing border around the bottom of the cake.

To make the fondant baby blanket:
Sprinkle your work surface with powdered sugar.

Using a flat wooden rolling pin, begin rolling about a ¼ pound of pink colored fondant. Turn it often so that it doesn't stick.

Continue rolling the fondant until it is flat and about 12" × 8".

Use a decorative "knit" textured rolling pin (available at Sweet Art) to inscribe the fondant surface with a knit blanket appearance.

Roll the design onto the fondant with the rolling pin in one smooth rolling move; do not pick up the rolling pin until you reach the end of the fondant.

Using a pizza wheel, cut the edges smooth to create about a 10" × 6" rectangle.

Use a scalloped edging tool to create the finished edges of the blanket.

To create the gathered look of the finished blanket:

Lay the fondant rectangle on a clean dish towel.

Begin gathering the dish towel and fondant into gentle folds.

Remove the fondant from the dish towel and gently gather the folds together about two inches from the top edge of the blanket.

Drape the blanket gently so that it looks like a real baby blanket and place it on the cake.

To make the buttercream baby booties:

1. Using a pastry tube with a #2E tip (it has lots of small openings for the knitted, ribbed look of the bootie), pipe the bootie toes onto a flat surface. Tip #4B would work, but not with quite the same effect.

2. Pipe a quantity of frosting onto the surface and finish with a slight downward swirl. Allow it to dry slightly.

3. For the top of the bootie, using the same tip, begin to pile the frosting upward from the slight swirl you left at the back of the "toe" of the bootie.

4. Finish with a tiny satin bow.

Repeat steps 1–4 to make the second bootie side-by-side with first.

Refrigerate the booties if the rest of the cake isn't ready for them to be placed yet.

Place the fondant blanket in the upper left corner of the cake, letting the edges hang delicately over the sides of the cake.

Using a spatula, gently remove the dried and finished booties from their surface and place them in the gathered part of the blanket.

Make buttercream roses and place them in the bottom right corner of the cake. Add one rose to the blanket in the gather just above the booties.

Place a square of parchment paper on the rose nail—keep it from slipping by affixing it with a dot of frosting in the center of the rose nail. (This will help you remove the rose from the nail later.)

Using round tip or open ended pastry bag, make a cone in the middle of the nail. This will support the center of the rose.

Using a #103 rose tube with the thick part pointing downward and thin part up, create each petal using a half circle wrist twist. Practice this until you get it right. Continue making rose petals, making each petal slightly larger than the last one until you have a completed rose.

Place roses on the cake.

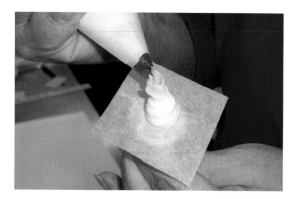

Using #65 leaf tip on a pastry bag filled with pastel green icing, pipe leaves directly on the cake around the roses.

Expert tip from Linda

If you have trouble following our directions here, and you really want to learn how to make a buttercream rose, which is pretty essential to cake decorating, take a short Wilton cake class at Michael's. Wilton's Yearbooks also have good instructions for this procedure.

Expert tip from Linda

Buttercream roses are about 50% butter, and butter is soft at room temperature. It hardens when it's chilled. You will want to make sure any decorative items made from buttercream are refrigerated until they are ready to be placed on your cake. In fact, you should keep your finished cakes in the refrigerator until they are ready to be served. They'll not only look better, they'll taste better, too. Refrigeration allows the flavors to meld together nicely.

Lift the rose off the parchment with scissors. Place it on the cake surface and slightly open the scissors and pull them away from the rose.

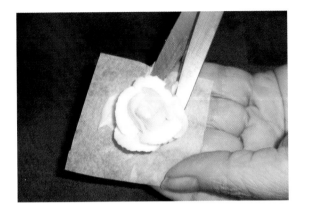

This cake can be adapted for a christening party with virtually no changes.
We've accessorized ours here with a rosary and a framed picture of the guest of honor.
Of course, you can choose any color for the roses and blanket, adapting it for a boy as well.

Silver Anniversary Cake

FOR THIS CAKE, OF COURSE we used the Silver Cake recipe on page 48. Nothing else would do.

You will need one recipe of the Silver Anniversary Cake and two batches of buttercream or cream cheese frosting. Bake the cake in two 8-inch round pans, let it cool, and then split the layers. Stack and fill with raspberry filling or lemon curd. Crumb coat with buttercream or cream cheese frosting and refrigerate the cake.

You will also need a one-inch wide silver ribbon about 36" long and a decorative bow made of the same ribbon.

When the icing is solid, remove the cake from the refrigerator and smooth coat it with a finishing layer of frosting.

On a piece of parchment paper, measure and mark out the amount of space you have for the large numerals on the top of the cake. We measured numerals that are five inches for the eight-inch cake shown here.

Using the marked paper as a guideline, sketch in the numbers with a pen or pencil.

Fill a pastry tube with white buttercream frosting and use a #12 tip. Pipe the frosting on following the sketched numbers. Put on the frosting good and thick.

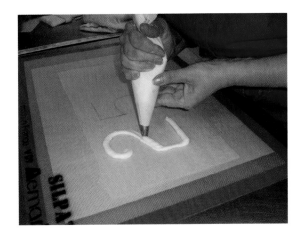

Freeze the numbers solid (at least two hours).

Remove the numbers from the freezer, and using a small straight spatula and fresh buttercream, fill in any gaps and make the edges smooth.

Run a spatula under each number to remove it from the parchment.

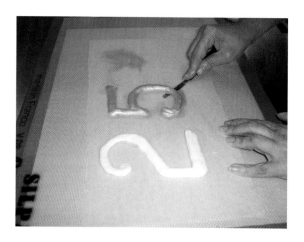

Dust the numbers with silver Luster Dust—food grade highlighting dust— available from Sweet Art Galleries or any cake decorating supplier.

Place the numbers on the cake while they are still frozen. If the cake isn't ready, put the numbers back in the freezer.

Fill a pastry tube with white frosting and make a decorative shell border along the top edge of cake and around the bottom of the cake.

For the bottom, use a pastry bag with shell tip #32 (an open star tip). Place the tip against the base of the cake at a 45 degree angle. Apply gentle pressure to the tube and with a slight up and down movement, pipe the frosting around the base of the cake, creating gentle little hills and valleys of border. Follow the directions for piping on a base border in Chapter 4 in the Bunny Cake instructions. We made this border a bit more flowing than that one, but you may make it in any way that is appealing to you; the main goal you should have for border creation is to make the border on each cake of a consistent size and to make the individual "puffs" of frosting evenly spaced. Practice, practice, practice.

Now make a border around the top edge of the cake, using white buttercream frosting and tip #2E to make a more frilly border.

Wrap the ribbon around the sides of the cake, an inch or so from the bottom and finish with the bow. Use gentle pressure to adhere the ribbon and bow to the frosting.

Refrigerate the cake until it is time to serve.

Violet Birthday Cake

YOU WILL NEED ONE RECIPE of the Silver Anniversary Cake on page 48 and two batches of buttercream or cream cheese frosting. Make the cake, let it cool, and then split the layers. For this cake, we simply stacked it using the buttercream frosting, but you may use any filling from Chapter 3 you like. Crumb coat with buttercream or cream cheese frosting and refrigerate.

You'll also need half a batch of buttercream frosting colored green with Americolor Gel paste food coloring, and another very small amount that is colored white or yellow for the violet centers. You will also need a narrow lavender ribbon for the trim.

While the cake is chilling, make one recipe of royal icing following the recipe on page 54. Using Americolor Gel paste food coloring, color it a deep purple. For more realistic looking violets, you could divide the icing and make varying shades of purple.

When the icing on the cake is firm, remove it from the refrigerator and smooth coat it with a finishing layer of frosting.

Using a pastry tube filled with white frosting and round tip #11, place little dots of frosting in a random pattern all over the surface of the cake. This creates what is called the "dotted Swiss" effect.

Using a shell tip, make a border around the base of the cake. Wrap the ribbon around the cake and tie a pretty bow on one side.

Return the cake to the freezer while you make your violets.

Place a piece of parchment paper on a clean work surface.

Using a #35 star-like flower tube tip and a pastry tube filled with the purple royal icing, hold the pastry bag at a right angle to the paper and touch the tip to the paper. Then squeeze gently, twist just a bit, and lift off the pastry tube. Keep making the violets like this on the parchment paper until you have several good ones. Squeezing icing out for a longer period of time and twisting more slowly will create larger violets. Make some in different sizes.

Allow the violets to air dry for a couple of hours. When the flowers are dry, use a small pastry tube with the end cut off, fill it with white or yellow royal or buttercream icing, and apply a dainty center to each flower.

Use a pastry tube with a #65 leaf tip and the green buttercream icing to make the leaves on the cake. Pile them kind of high in places to make a sort of "bed" for the violets to rest on. Put some on the sides of the cake too. Then just use the leaves as the glue that holds the violets in place. Carefully pick up each violet and fit it into place on the bed of leaves.

Refrigerate this cake until it is time to serve.

Expert tip from Linda

You could also use pink royal icing to make forget-me-nots in this same manner.

Tea Cakes

FOR THESE, YOU'LL NEED TWO sheet cakes made using either the Silver Cake recipe on page 48 or the Golden Chiffon Cake recipe on page 49.

Stack the two sheet cakes; we used raspberry filling for ours, but you could make them with lemon curd or buttercream frosting.

Measure and cut the cake, as you did for the petits fours in Chapter 4, but these should be about twice the size and height of the petits fours. We cut ours to 2" × 2", and they are about 2" high stacked. Crumb coat each cake on all sides with buttercream and refrigerate.

Sprinkle your work surface with powdered sugar and roll out about 8 ounces of fondant. Color the fondant with a drop or two of Americolor Gel food coloring to the shade you choose. Ours here are a very, very pale green and yellow.

Run a spatula under the fondant as you work to loosen it from the work surface so that it won't tear as you lift it to place it on the cake.

Use a large soft brush to brush off loose sugar from the bottom of the fondant.

Trim the sides evenly.

Drape the fondant over the cake, tenting it loosely.

116

When working with square cakes such as these, you want to attach the corners first.

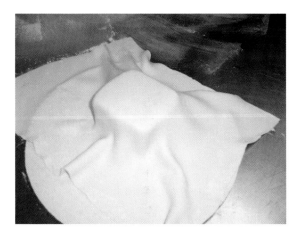

Pull out, stretching the fondant away from the cake. Do not push in.

After the corners are attached, pull the remaining fondant out from the sides. Press in with a very soft touch, working toward the center from each corner.

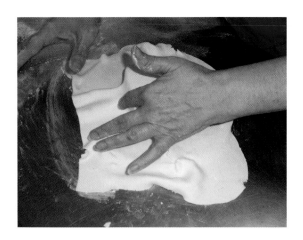

If the fondant tears, work it back together.

Once you have the cake entirely covered with fondant, remove the excess fondant by cutting it off square with a sharp knife.

If necessary, use a small amount of buttercream frosting to repair any tears, smoothing it all over with a small spatula.

Use any of an assortment of butterfly molds, cookie cutters, and lace molds to make the butterflies.

Make your butterflies using whichever method works best for you. We used the small butterfly mold.

Before trimming the molded butterflies, paint them with yellow Luster Dust, available from Sweet Art or any cake decorating supply store. For the cakes shown in this section, we trimmed our yellow butterflies with brown Luster Dust to match some of the butterflies on our serving plates. Take your inspiration from the dishes you will use to serve your cakes, especially if they are as pretty as these.

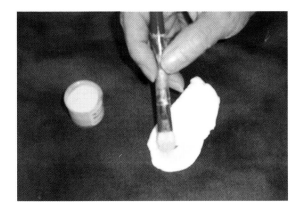

Trim the butterfly neatly with a utility knife.

Make two butterflies for each tea cake.

Affix each butterfly to the cake at an angle, using buttercream frosting to hold it in place.

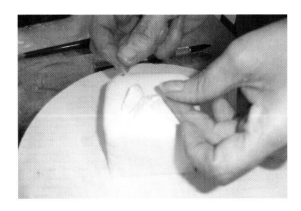

Let it dry.

Cut a small roll of fondant to create the body of the butterfly and affix it to middle of the wings. You can leave this white or paint it first with Luster Dust. (We made ours brown.)

To make the ribbon on the "package," roll out about ⅛ pound of fondant—don't worry about waste—use more than you need because any excess can be returned to the container.

After you roll out the fondant, to add more interest to the fondant ribbons and bows, you could create a design in the ribbon by using a textured rolling pin. Do this to the whole piece of fondant before you cut it into strips for the ribbons and bows.

Use a ruler and a pizza wheel to cut the fondant into ribbons and place them on the cake to create the look of wrapped gift package.

To make the loops of the bow, roll a small piece of fondant to about ⅛" thickness. Cut small strips crosswise from this piece.

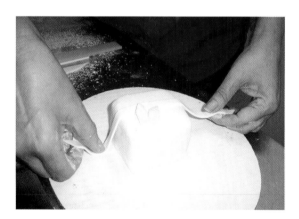

Form each small strip into a loop.

Set the loops on their sides and allow them to dry.
Continue working until you have several loops,
enough to put about six on each tea cake.

 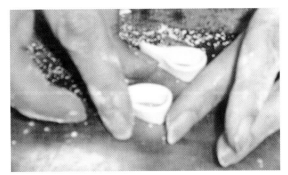

Arrange the loops on the cakes so that they look like bows on the ribbons.

Bridal Shower Cupcakes

CUPCAKES ARE GREAT—easy to make, easy to remove from the pan, no stacking necessary—no wonder they are so popular. The bridal shower cupcakes shown on this page are just one of hundreds of cupcake ideas you'll think of as these little gems emerge from your oven.

Use the Silver Cake, Tawny Torte, Red Velvet Cake, or the Golden Chiffon Cake recipes from Chapter 3. Spray cupcake tins with cooking spray and line with pastel-colored paper liners. Give these a light coating with the cooking spray, too. Fill each cupcake mold about ⅔ full of batter and bake about 20 minutes or until a toothpick inserted in the center of a cupcake comes out clean. (Use oven settings for each recipe as directed in Chapter 3.)

To decorate these cupcakes, you will need about 32 ounces of fondant. We used Choco-Pan, available from Sweet Art Galleries (www.choco-pan.com), but you can use any brand you like or make your own.

Real life tip from Sandy

You can make fondant yourself, although it's a chore you may not want to concern yourself with at this stage of your career as a cake decorator. I've tasted Linda's Choco-Pan®, it is really good, and you can buy it from Sweet Art Galleries, but we have included a recipe in Chapter 3 if you'd like to make your own.

Leave half of it white. Color the remaining 16 ounces half pink and half yellow. Use gel paste food color to color the fondant. We recommend Americolor Gel paste color, available from Sweet Art, for coloring fondant. Make it as pale pastel or as full vibrant color as you want. Gel paste color is best for coloring fondant because it mixes easily and the fondant maintains its texture. Using liquid food coloring could add too much moisture to the fondant, so that it wouldn't hold its shape as well.

The amounts of frosting required are approximate, of course, depending on how many cupcakes you bake. We overestimate. It is better to have too much than too little, and none of the fondant will be wasted because you can save it to use in other projects.

You'll need about a cup of white buttercream frosting and another half cup, colored green.

Cool the cupcakes in pans for about five minutes and then turn them out onto a clean dishcloth. Set each cupcake upright and allow to cool to room temperature.

Frost each cupcake smooth with buttercream frosting.

Roll the white fondant out smooth with a regular wooden rolling pin. Sprinkle the work surface with powdered sugar to keep the fondant from sticking. Turn it several times as you roll it out smooth. (See the instructions for rolling, shaping, cutting, and texturing fondant in the Baby Shower and Christening Cake section earlier in this chapter.)

Texture the fondant with a textured rolling pin. A variety of these textured pins are available at Sweet Art Galleries, and several are appropriate for this project. We used the "rose and daisy" for this cake.

Use a cookie cutter or fondant cutter to cut small rounds of the textured fondant. Place one round atop each buttercream frosted cupcake.

Apply a buttercream leaf with green icing, using a pastry tube and tip #65, to each fondant round. Apply slight pressure and pull the leaf off to a point. Practice this on parchment paper until you have the hang of creating the kind of leaf you want.

Cut daisies with the daisy plunger (PME plunger set, available at Sweet Art) from the yellow fondant.

Place daisies carefully on the buttercream leaf.

On the DVD-ROM that accompanies this book, Linda takes you step-by-step through the process of creating a fondant rose. Follow along with Linda on the DVD and make roses from the pink fondant frosting. Place a rose and a daisy on some of the cupcakes and two daisies on others. We used the serving plate as inspiration for our theme of roses and daisies, carrying it through to the textured fondant topper for the cupcakes and the flowers added to each cupcake, maintaining our theme throughout. You might even want to include a bouquet of real pink roses and yellow daisies on the table when you serve these cupcakes.

Christmas Cupcakes

TO MAKE THE GLITTER SNOWFLAKE cupcakes with blue frosting, you'll need one recipe of buttercream frosting, colored blue, and eight ounces of white fondant. You'll also need some silver or white edible glitter, available from CK Products (www.ckproducts.com).

Spread blue buttercream frosting on cupcakes.

Sprinkle with edible white or silver glitter.

Using a snowflake cutter, available at CK Products or Ateco (www.atecousa.com), cut snowflakes from rolled out white fondant.

Sprinkle with edible white or silver glitter.

To make the green holly cupcakes, you'll need one recipe of white buttercream frosting, a large pastry tube with tip #2D, a small pastry tube full of red buttercream frosting, and about six ounces of green fondant.

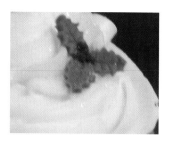

Using pastry tube with a 2D (large star) tip, pipe buttercream frosting in a spiral atop each cupcake.

Use the holly cutter, available from Sweet Art (PME plunger set), to cut out holly leaves from the green fondant.

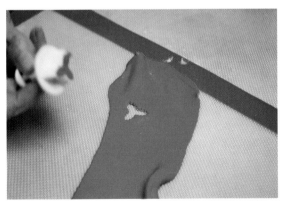

Arrange the holly leaves on the frosted cupcakes.

Use red buttercream and pipe on berries with small paper bag—no tip.

Sprinkle with edible glitter.

That's it! Two easy decorating methods to make holiday cupcakes. Vary the color combinations and techniques to fit your holiday color scheme.

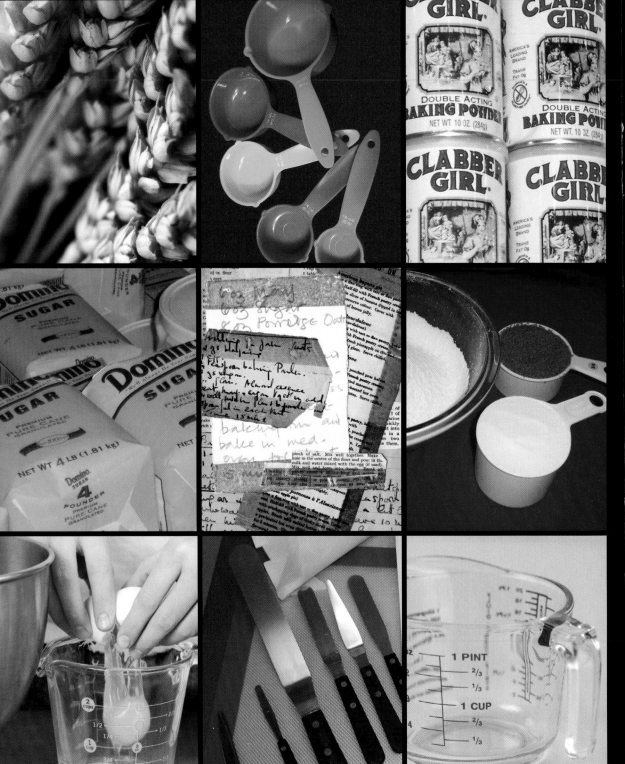

A

Things That Are Good To Know

The English are as fond of baking as we Americans, and although many terms are interchangeable, the language does differ from one side of the Atlantic to the other. So here, for the benefit of both, is a short glossary of baking terms.

U.S. English	British English
Extra fine sugar	castor sugar
Powdered or confectioners' sugar	icing sugar
Plastic wrap	clingfilm
Cornstarch	cornflour
Light brown sugar	demerara sugar
Heavy cream	double cream
Light cream	single cream
Cupcakes	fairy cakes
Bread flour	strong flour
All purpose flour	plain flour
Self-rising flour	self-raising flour
Extracts	Essences
Shortening	White Vegetable Fat

In addition:

Granulated sugar is coarser than in the U.S., not suitable for baking.
Golden syrup is similar to corn syrup.

Check the manufacturer's instructions for your oven and make sure it is level. An uneven cooking surface can negatively affect your baked goods too.

Real life tip from Sandy

Always preheat your oven. Make sure it has reached the desired temperature before you place the cake into the oven.

Measurement Conversions

It's easy to convert pints to liters, tablespoons to ounces, and Fahrenheit to Celsius if you know the multiplier to use. If you don't, here are a few handy measurement conversions that will get you through most cake recipes.

Liquid Measurements

Measurement	Liquid Equivalent	Metric
1 teaspoon		5 milliliters
1 tablespoon	1/2 ounce	15 milliliters
1/4 cup	2 ounces	59 milliliters
1/3 cup	2 2/3 ounces	79 milliliters
1/2 cup	4 ounces	118 milliliters
3/4 cup	6 ounces	177 milliliters
1 cup	8 ounces (1/2 pint)	237 milliliters

Dry Measurements

Measurement	Dry equivalent	Metric
1 ounce	1/16 pound	30 grams
2 ounces	1/8 pound	55 grams
3 ounces	3/16 pound	85 grams
4 ounces	1/4 pound	125 grams
8 ounces	1/2 pound	240 grams
12 ounces	3/4 pound	375 grams
16 ounces	1 pound	454 grams
1 kilogram	2.2 pounds	1000 grams

Oven Temperature Conversion Chart

Fahrenheit	Celsius	Gas Mark
225°	110°	1/4
250°	130°	1/2
275°	140°	1
300°	150°	2
325°	170°	3
350°	180°	4
375°	190°	5
400°	200°	6
425°	220°	7
450°	230°	8

When setting the temperature of your oven, bear in mind that oven thermostats may vary or be "off" just a bit. Other things such as heat, humidity, and altitude can affect baking times and temperatures too, so pay attention to the results you get and be ready to adjust the temperature or baking time to compensate for these differences.

Measuring Techniques

To measure flour, sift flour once before measuring. Then spoon lightly into a measuring cup and level off with a spatula.

To measure sugar, fill the measuring cup with granulated sugar and level off with a spatula.

To measure brown sugar, pack the sugar firmly into the cup. Level with a spatula. To easily remove brown sugar from the measuring cup, tap the cup lightly so that the sugar falls out in one solid chunk.

To measure baking powder, soda, salt, and spices, fill the measuring spoon full and level off with a spatula.

To measure shortening, pack the shortening firmly into the cup and level off with a spatula. Hold the cup sideways under a thin stream of hot water to loosen the shortening so that it slips easily out of the measuring cup.

To measure liquids, use a glass measuring cup. Set it on the counter and bend to bring your eye level with the cup. Watch through the side as you fill the cup to the desired measurement with the liquid. Do not try to "eyeball" this from above. The top line of the liquid will appear distorted from a top view.

Use medium to large eggs. Let them come to room temperature before using. When separating the yolk from the white, make sure no yolk gets into the egg white. If the white contains even the tiniest amount of yolk, it won't beat to a stiff foam.

Troubleshooting Guide

Here is a list of things that can go wrong with your cakes during baking and possible things to adjust to correct the problem:

Problem	Possible Causes
Hard top crust	Oven temperature too high
	Overbaking
Sticky top crust	Too much sugar
	Cake didn't bake long enough
Humped or cracked crust	Too much flour or too little liquid
	Cake was mixed too long
	Batter not spread evenly in pan
	Oven temperature too high
One side higher than the other	Batter not spread evenly
	Uneven pan
	Pan too close to side of oven
	Oven rack or stove not level
	Uneven oven heat
Soggy layer at bottom	Too much liquid
	Underbeaten eggs
	Shortening too soft
	Cake wasn't mixed long enough
	Cake wasn't baked long enough
Cake falls	Too much sugar, liquid, leavening, or shortening
	Too little flour
	Oven temperature too low
	Cake didn't bake long enough

Problem	Possible Causes
Coarse grain	Use of all purpose flour when cake flour was called for
	Too much leavening
	Shortening too soft
	Shortening and sugar weren't creamed well enough
	Cake wasn't mixed long enough
	Oven temperature too low
Tough Crumb	Too much flour
	Too many eggs
	Too little shortening or sugar
	Cake was mixed too long
	Oven temperature too high
Cake feels heavy, too compact	Too much liquid or shortening
	Too many eggs
	Too little leavening or flour
	Cake was mixed too long
	Oven temperature too high
Crumbly, falling apart cake	Too much sugar, leavening, or shortening
	Cake wasn't mixed long enough
	Improper pan treatment
	Improper cooling

Real life tip from Sandy

Don't crowd cake pans into your oven. A typical wire oven shelf will hold two or three round cake pans comfortably. Do not place one cake pan above another in the oven. Baking cakes requires an even flow of heat around the oven, and overloading the oven with cake pans impedes this flow.

B

The Fondant Class on DVD

Ever wanted to take a cake decorating class, learn how to work with fondant to make those gorgeous cakes that look like marble statuary, the kind you aren't even sure you're supposed to eat? Slip the DVD that accompanies this book into your DVD player, sit back, relax, and watch as Linda Shonk, A.C.F.-certified Executive Pastry Chef, leads you through the steps required to make a beautiful fondant covered confection you might never believe you could make. But it's really easy to learn how when Chef Linda walks you through each step, carefully explaining and demonstrating as she cuts out fondant daisies, creates a fondant rose, and enrobes a two-layer cake in fondant using Choco-Pan®, Chef Linda's own creation, which has made a lasting impression on the world of sugar art and cake decorating.

S HE TELLS YOU WHAT SHE'S doing as she demonstrates how to do it, and she throws in a few of those little secrets and techniques that all chefs know but few share with beginners.

Watching this 49-minute DVD (with a retail value of $44.95) is like attending one of Linda's classes in cake decorating. She truly loves what she does, and she loves sharing it with her students at Ivy Tech College and with you, as you attend the class on this DVD.

Watch as Linda makes roses, daisies, and leaves from Choco-Pan®.

Learning how to make these roses is one of the features of the DVD.

Watch as Linda demonstrates how to use JEM tools to create an easy fondant border.

Linda leads you step by step through all the processes required to create this beautiful cake.

Watch the DVD as many times as you want as you master each step. Learn at your own pace and keep the DVD handy so you can refer to it again and again as you work to duplicate Linda's style of decorating.

Once you've mastered the techniques Linda demonstrates on this DVD, you'll be turning out masterpieces of your own design in no time. And by using the recipes in Chapter 3 of this book, your cakes will be famous for not only looking good but tasting incredibly good too!

Index

Purchase Choco-Pan® and the other innovative products used to create the professional quality designs featured in *Picture Yourself Decorating Cakes*!

Developed by co-author and award-winning culinary artist and instructor Linda Shonk, Choco-Pan® is the easy to use, great tasting alternative to rolled fondant. It is made with only the highest quality ingredients including the finest white and dark chocolates available. Those chocolates enhance the flavor of Choco-Pan® while giving it a level of pliability that remains unmatched by any other cake covering on the market. Choco-Pan® can also be used to accent pastries and cookies, cover tea cakes, fill candies, etc. Your customers will love the taste of Choco-Pan® and will ask for it by name! Don't miss the opportunity for your beautiful cakes to taste as good as they look… order Choco-Pan® today!

Also available through Sweet Art, Inc.:

- Pâte à glacer
- Textured rolling pins
- Luster dust
- And much more!

Order online today at www.choco-pan.com or contact Sweet Art, Inc.

Sweet Art, Inc.
6011 E. Hanna Avenue, Suite E | Indianapolis, IN 46203
317.787.3647 (phone) | 317.787.3702 (fax) | 888.287.8455 (toll free)

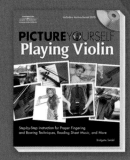

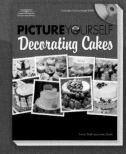